THE LONDON UNDERGROUND SERIAL KILLER

GEOFF PLATT

PEN & SWORD
TRUE CRIME

First published in Great Britain in 2015 by
Pen & Sword True Crime
an imprint of
Pen & Sword Books Ltd
47 Church Street
Barnsley
South Yorkshire
S70 2AS

Copyright © Geoff Platt 2015

ISBN 978 1 47382 732 5

Typeset in Plantin by
Mac Style Ltd, Bridlington, East Yorkshire
Printed and bound in the UK by CPI Group (UK) Ltd,
Croydon, CR0 4YY

Pen & Sword Books Ltd incorporates the imprints of Pen &
Sword Archaeology, Atlas, Aviation, Battleground, Discovery,
Family History, History, Maritime, Military, Naval, Politics,
Railways, Select, Transport, True Crime, and Fiction,
Frontline Books, Leo Cooper, Praetorian Press, Seaforth
Publishing and Wharncliffe.

For a complete list of Pen & Sword titles please contact
PEN & SWORD BOOKS LIMITED
47 Church Street, Barnsley, South Yorkshire, S70 2AS,
England
E-mail: enquiries@pen-and-sword.co.uk
Website: www.pen-and-sword.co.uk

Contents

CHAPTER 1

The Introduction

A recent visit to a local bookshop revealed the public interest in serial killers, their victims, their motives, and what separates them from 'ordinary people'. At the end of the section on 'Crime', there are now rows and rows of books under the heading, 'True Crime'. There are books written by psychologists, criminologists, sociologists and even some written by, or on behalf of, the persons convicted of these crimes, but there are few written by police officers. In fact, research now reveals that 'True Crime' is the fastest-growing area in book sales.

Psychologists, criminologists and sociologists differentiate between 'mass killers', 'spree killers' and 'serial killers'. They are academics and like to have definitions to work by. A researcher investigating serial killers does not want to talk to mass killers or spree killers. If the definition of a serial killer is someone who has killed five people, then there is no point in talking to anyone who has killed two, three or four people as they will now be in prison, where they will be prevented from ever killing a fifth person and thereby qualifying to be a serial killer.

In fact, the universal definition of a serial killer is "Someone who has been convicted of five or more murders." This means that academics have to wait until after the trial so that they can classify the killers before talking to them, but by that time the killers have regained their self-control, their self-assurance and usually, their silence. They are then very likely to be detained in a prison or a mental hospital and they may very well be taking pills to make them more manageable.

Authors and journalists sell their wares on sensationalism. 'Serial killer' is an emotive term that arouses our interest. Some researchers have claimed to have identified as many as sixty serial killers in the United Kingdom, but according to a strict classification there are only eleven:

Robert Black (active between 1969 and 1986)
John Childs (active between 1974 and 1978)
Kenneth Erskine (active in 1988)
John George Haigh (active between 1940 and 1949)
Colin Ireland (active between 1990 and 1993)
Peter Thomas Anthony Manuel (active between 1956 and 1958)
Dennis Andrew Nilsen (active between 1978 and 1983)
Peter William Sutcliffe (active between 1976 and 1981)
Rosemary West (active between 1967 and 1979)
Steven Gerald James Wright (active in 2006)
Dr Harold Shipman (active between 1974 and 1998)

The most startling omissions from this list are:

William Burke and William Hare (The Body Snatchers) (active between January and December 1828); Ian Brady and Myra Hyndley (The Moors Murderers)(active between 1963 and 1965); Frederick West (active from 1967 and 1979)(The Cromwell Street Killers) (although his wife Rosemary West is on the list)

The reasons for these omissions are that Hare was allowed to turn King's Evidence against Burke and was not convicted of Murder. Brady and Hindley killed 'just' four children and Fred West committed suicide whilst awaiting trial and was not, therefore, convicted.

These statistics are, like many statistics, affected by a range of factors that make them almost meaningless:

1. The existence of the death penalty before 1965 meant that as soon as a person was convicted of their first Murder they were rushed off to the scaffold and executed within weeks, so that nobody was ever convicted of five Murders.
2. People who do murder five people, have lost all respect for human life, including their own, and frequently commit suicide rather than face humiliation, conviction and life imprisonment.
3. People who have murdered five people, know the best way to deal with witnesses.

4. Trials are expensive and the DPP and the CPS usually stop prosecuting at two Murders. Therefore only those seeking infamy and who plead guilty are ever convicted of five Murders.
5. Many serial killers are dealt with under Mental Health Act legislation and therefore avoid trial and conviction.
6. For obvious reasons, many serial killers keep moving and move between criminal jurisdictions. When they are finally arrested the jurisdiction where they are arrested tends not to let them go, even for another trial in another jurisdiction.

Perhaps, in the light of these weaknesses, the definition of a serial killer needs to be re-written? Perhaps the fact that a Law Officer of the Crown has determined that there is sufficient evidence to justify charging a person with five Murders should be enough? There is certainly no reason why committing suicide whilst awaiting trial/ being sent to a mental institution/ pleading 'Not Guilty' should allow a person to evade the list. If this data is going to assist psychologists, sociologists and criminologists to advise our politicians as to the best way to reduce serial killing, do we not owe it to ourselves to make the data that they work with more accurate, in order that their results are more accurate?

Kieran Patrick Kelly had killed his sixteenth and last victim in his cell at Clapham Police Station. Only ten minutes after he had killed, he was taken out of the cell and interviewed by two very senior officers in my presence. This is highly unusual, perhaps unique. Nobody else has ever spoken to a serial killer so soon after the moment he has killed. He was loaded with testosterone and adrenaline, mentally, physically and sexually aroused and could not stop talking about what he had done. He was asked if he had murdered his cellmate and he admitted that he had, and, unprompted, he then went on to admit that he had also previously killed fifteen other people. There being no evidence to support this claim, the police officers refused to accept his story and Kelly had to work very hard to convince them that he was telling the truth. He just kept talking …

Over the next two years, Kelly was detained in solitary confinement in order to prevent him from killing any more cellmates. Almost the only person that he was allowed to speak to was me, Acting Detective Constable Geoff Platt, the officer selected to carry out the day-to-day investigation of the sixteen Murders that Kelly had admitted. Kelly had little choice about who he talked to, it was me or nobody.

The story of Kelly and the Murders on the Northern Line were actively suppressed by Press Officers working for the Government. They felt that stories about a man discretley wandering around and pushing people under underground trains for no reason would instil fear in the public and reduce the numbers using the London Underground.

Passengers refusing to use the underground would then need to find other ways to get to work, such as train or bus, thus overloading these systems and causing widespread panic. London goes into meltdown every time that there is a one-day tube strike. It would be much worse if the fear induced an indefinite problem and the London Underground was rendered useless, because nobody wanted to use it. Perhaps it was best to put a lid on this story?

It is only natural that a subject that periodically features at the top of our television news programmes, and then fills the front pages of our national press, but about which none of us has any knowledge or experience, should fascinate us and stimulate us to want to find out more.

It is German Police Inspector Ernst Gennat who is widely credited with creating the concept of serial killers in 1930, but there were a lot of other things happening in Germany in the 1930s and the concept was largely overlooked and ignored amongst the chaos. It was not until the 1970s that FBI Special Agent Robert Ressler drew attention to the concept and created the term "serial killer".

A serial killer is, traditionally, a person who has murdered a certain number of people over a period of more than a month, with down time, sometimes called a "cooling off period", between the murders. Different individuals or agencies specify that two, three, four or five people need to be killed to make the suspect a serial killer.

There are generally accepted to have been sixty acknowledged serial killers in the United Kingdom. Because the Crown

Prosecution Service (CPS), who had received police reports on all sixteen murders admitted by Kelly, and who had originally decided to charge him with five murders, decided to stop prosecuting Kelly once he had been convicted of two murders, and because HM Government gave instructions to the Metropolitan Police to restrict publicity about a serial killer on the London Underground, fearing that it would promote public panic, Kelly is seldom included in the list of British serial killers, despite the fact that he is suspected of murdering more people than anyone other than Dr Harold Shipman.

No.	Facts	Serial Killer?	Convicted?	Suspected?
1.	Stephen Akinmurele (also known as the "Cul-de-sac killer") had a pathological hatred of old people. He was charged by Police with the murder of five elderly people in Blackpool and the Isle of Man between 1995 and 1998 and the officers who investigated the case suspected him of two further murders. Akinmurele committed suicide whilst detained in Strangeways Prison whilst on remand awaiting trial and was never convicted and therefore, technically, does not meet the criteria for a serial killer.	No	0	7
2.	Beverley Allitt (also known as the "Angel of Death") was convicted of killing four babies and injuring at least nine others over a period of 59 days between February and April 1991 in the children's ward at Grantham and Kesteven Hospital, Lincolnshire, where Allitt was employed as a State Enrolled Nurse. She was sentenced to Life Imprisonment in 1991. Having been convicted of "only" killing four babies, Allitt also technically fails to meet the criteria to become a serial killer.	No	4	4
3.	Levi Bellfield (also known as the "Bus Stop Stalker") murdered Amanda (Millie) Dowler in 2002 and went on to commit two more fatal hammer attacks on young women in South West London in 2003 and 2004. He was convicted of three murders and one attempted murder and has been sentenced to a whole life term. He is suspected of several more attacks on young women. Having been convicted of "only" three murders, Bellfield also technically fails to meet the criteria to become a serial killer.	No	3	3+
4.	Robert Black was convicted of the kidnap and murder of four girls aged between 5 and 11 years between 1981 and 1986. He is also suspected of unsolved child murders across Europe dating back to 1969. On 19 May 1994 at Newcastle upon Tyne Moot Hall, Black was found guilty on all counts, was sentenced to Life Imprisonment, and told that he was should serve at least 35 years. While still in prison, on 16 December 2009, Black was charged with the murder of Jennifer Cardy. He was found guilty on 27 October 2011 and was given a further life sentence by Armagh Crown Court. Black is, therefore, the first person on this list to qualify as a serial killer, although a quarter of a century had lapsed since he was regularly murdering people and of interest to researchers.	Yes	5	5+

No.		No		
5. and	Ian Brady and Myra Hindley (also known as the "Moors Murderers") murdered five children, aged between 10 and 17, between July 1963 and October 1965, and buried them on Saddleworth	No	3	5
6.	Moor, near Manchester. On 6 May 1966 Brady and Hindley were convicted of three murders and sentenced to Life Imprisonment, as the death penalty had been withdrawn whilst they were on remand for the murders. On 1 July 1987 the body of a fourth victim was discovered and Brady and Hindley admitted the murder, but the Crown Prosecution Service declined to prosecute on the grounds that no additional penalty was likely to be imposed and a further trial may assist the accused to make a public confession that would indicate remorse and possibly assist their applications for parole. Hindley died in prison on 15 November 2002 of Bronchial Pneumonia. Accordingly, neither Brady nor Hindley ever qualified to be classified as serial killers.			
7.	Mary Ann Britland had mice infest her home in Ashton-Under-Lyne in February 1886. She went to the chemist's and bought some packets of "Harrison's Vermin Killer". As this contained both strychnine and arsenic, she was required to sign the poison register. The next month she murdered her daughter and then after another month she murdered her husband and a couple of weeks later she murdered her lover's wife. On each occasion, Britland claimed an insurance pay-out. Following her trial at Manchester Assizes, she was hanged at Strangeways Prison in Manchester on 9 August 1886. Having "only" been convicted of three murders, Britland does not meet the definition of a serial killer.	No	3	3
8.	Peter Bryan was institutionalised for a fatal hammer attack on a woman in 1993, re-apprehended for cannibalising a friend in 2004, but able to batter a fellow patient to death months later. On 15 March 2005 at the Old Bailey, Bryan pleaded guilty to two counts of Manslaughter on the grounds of diminished responsibility and was sentenced to Life Imprisonment. A conviction for two counts of Manslaughter does not meet the requirements for classification as a serial killer.	No	2	3

No.	Facts	Serial Killer?	Convicted?	Suspected?
9 and	William Burke and William Hare (popularly known as Burke and Hare) were notorious body snatchers in Edinburgh in 1828. Assisted by Burke's mistress, Helen McDougall, and Hare's wife, Margaret Laird, they delivered sixteen dead bodies to Dr Robert Knox at the Edinburgh Medical School. As medical science flourished, the demand for cadavers rose sharply but the main source, the bodies of executed criminals, dried up owing to a reduction in the number of executions. Burke and Hare met the demand, firstly by grave-robbing from local cemeteries but, as security improved and they gained in confidence, they started killing vagrants for the fees that they received at the Medical School. Eventually, Burke, Hare and McDougall were each charged with three Murders, but the case against them was considered weak. The Lord Advocate invited Hare, who was not considered to be very bright, to give King's Evidence to convict the others in exchange for his own release. Burke was convicted and hanged. Hare spent the rest of his life running away from violent mobs trying to impose a similar, but unlawful, penalty on him. A conviction for just three murders did not qualify any of those responsible qualifying to be serial killers.	No	Burke 3	<16
10.			Hare 0	<16
11.	George Chapman was born Severin Antoniovich Klosowski in Nargornak in Poland, and later moved to London. Between 1901 and 1903, he killed three of his wives by administering tartar-emetic and was arrested. With routine executions for relatively minor offences being the norm at this time, the law did not allow an indictment to contain more than one charge of Murder as those convicted could only be executed once. Chapman was therefore charged only with the murder of Maud Marsh. He was convicted on March 19, 1903, and hanged at Wandsworth Prison on April 7, 1903. He is suspected by some authors of being Jack the Ripper. A single conviction for Murder does not qualify Chapman as a serial killer.	No	3	<15

No.	Description			
12.	John Childs was an active armed robber, who was arrested by the Metropolitan Police Flying Squad in 1979. He turned Queens Evidence and admitted working as a serial killer between 1974 and 1978. Despite none of the bodies ever having been found, he was convicted in 1979 of six contract killings and became known as the most prolific hit man in the UK. He implicated two others in the murders, but they were released in 2003 after a judge ruled Childs to be a "pathological liar". On 4 December 1979 at the Old Bailey, Childs was convicted and sentenced to six concurrent life sentences and a whole life term. Accordingly, Childs becomes the second serial killer in this list.	Yes	6	6
13.	John Reginald Halliday Christie lived at 10 Rillington Place, Notting Hill, London, with the Evans family as his tenants. When, in 1949, Beryl Evans and her daughter Geraldine were found strangled, Christie was a key prosecution witness and Beryl's husband, Timothy, was charged with both murders, convicted of his daughter's murder and hanged. Christie moved out of Rillington Place in March 1953, and shortly afterwards the bodies of three other women were discovered hidden in an alcove in the kitchen and Christie's wife's body was found beneath the floorboards in the front room. Christie was arrested, convicted of his wife's murder and hanged. He committed his murders between 1943 and 1953, usually by strangling his victims after he had rendered them unconscious with domestic gas; some he raped as they lay unconscious. The miscarriage of justice led to the abolition of capital punishment. Despite the evidence against him, Christie was charged with just one Murder and does not therefore qualify as a serial killer.	No	1	6
14.	Dr Robert George Clements was from Belfast in Northern Ireland and worked in Lancashire as a physician and surgeon. He was suspected of the murder of his fourth wife, who died of morphine poisoning. His first three wives also predeceased him, raising suspicions that he had murdered them too. Clements committed suicide with an overdose of morphine before he was caught by the police and never stood trial. He does not, therefore, qualify as a serial killer.	No	0	4

No.	Facts	Serial Killer?	Convicted?	Suspected?
15.	John Cooper (also known as "The Wildman"; and "The Bullseye Killer") burgled a three-storey farmhouse in Scoveston Park in Milford Haven on 22 December 1985, shooting and killing brother and sister, Richard and Helen Thomas and later burning down the house. In 1989 Cooper used the same shotgun to gun down Peter and Gwenda Dixon whilst they were taking a walk on a coastal path. In September 2011 he was convicted of all four murders and sentenced to Life Imprisonment, but this is not enough to define him as a serial killer.	No	4	4
16.	Mary Ann Cotton (née Robson) is sometimes claimed to have been Britain's first serial killer. She was believed to have murdered up to 21 people, including her own children, mainly by arsenic poisoning. Mary Ann Cotton was hanged at Durham County Gaol on 24 March 1873, but as the law at this time only allowed a single indictment for Murder, she technically does not qualify as a serial killer.	No	1	<21?
17.	Dr Thomas Neill Cream (also known as the Lambeth Poisoner) was a Scottish–Canadian serial killer, who claimed his first proven victims in the United States and the rest in England, with others possibly in Canada and Scotland. Cream, who poisoned his victims, was hanged on 15 November 1892 at Newgate Prison, but as the law at this time only allowed a single indictment for Murder, he technically does not qualify as a serial killer.	No	1	<10?
18.	Dale Christopher Cregan is a convicted drug-dealer from Manchester who on 25 May 2012, in a public house in Droylsden, shot dead a rival and tried to kill three other men. Two months later he killed the first victim's father in Clayton by shooting him and throwing a hand grenade at him. The next month he made an emergency call to the police, and Constables Nicola Hughes, 23, and Fiona Bone, 32, responded to it. When they arrived, Cregan shot them and threw an M75 hand grenade at them. Both officers were hit by at least eight bullets as Cregan fired 32 shots in 31 seconds. He was sentenced to a whole life term of imprisonment, for the four Murders, but does not qualify as a serial killer.	No	4	4

#	Description			
19.	Frederick Bailey Deeming was responsible for the murder of his first wife Marie, and his four children, at Rainhill, Merseyside, on or about 26 July 1891, and a second wife, Emily Mather, at Windsor, Melbourne, Australia on 24 December 1891. Less than three months elapsed between the discovery of Mather's body in Windsor, Melbourne, in March 1892, and Deeming's execution for her murder in May 1892. As the law at this time only allowed a single indictment for Murder, he technically does not qualify as a serial killer.	No	1	6
20.	Joanna Dennehy set out on a killing spree in Peterborough and Hereford in March 2013 with the assistance of three men, who were believed to be her sexual partners. When the bodies of three men, who had died from stab wounds to the heart, were found in ditches around Peterborough, Dennehy was arrested, convicted and sentenced to a whole life term of imprisonment. Dennehy does not qualify as a serial killer.	No	3	3
21 and 22.	John Duffy and David Mulcahy (also known as the 'Railway Rapists' and the 'Railway Killers') are two British rapists and serial killers who together attacked numerous women at railway stations in the south of England between 1982 and 1986. Duffy went on trial in February 1988 and was convicted of two murders and four rapes. Mulcahy was convicted of three murders and seven rapes and handed three life sentences, with a 30-year recommendation. Later Duffy was convicted of 17 more rapes and received a further 12 years imprisonment. Neither was convicted of the five Murders required to qualify as a serial killer.	No	Duffy 2 Mulcahy 3	
23.	Amelia Elizabeth Dyer (née Hobley) was the most prolific baby farm murderer of Victorian England. She was tried and hanged for one murder, but there is little doubt she was responsible for many more similar deaths, possibly 400 or more, over a period of perhaps twenty years. She was hanged at Newgate Prison on Wednesday, 10 June 1896, but does not qualify as a serial killer.	No	1	400
24.	Kenneth Erskine (also known as the "Stockwell Strangler") murdered at least seven elderly people by breaking into their homes and strangling them. He frequently sexually assaulted them. He was convicted of murdering seven pensioners in 1988 and sentenced to Life Imprisonment, with a recommendation that he serve 40 years. Since his conviction Erskine has been assessed as mentally disordered and transferred to Broadmoor Hospital for the criminally insane, but his seven convictions for Murder remain and he qualifies as a serial killer.	Yes	7	7+

No.	Facts	Serial Killer?	Convicted?	Suspected?
25 and 26.	Catherine Flannagan and Margaret Higgins (also known as the "Black Widows of Liverpool") were Irish sisters who were convicted of poisoning and murdering one person in Liverpool and suspected of more deaths. The women collected a burial society pay-out, a type of life insurance, on each death, and it was eventually found that they had been committing murders using arsenic to obtain the insurance money. Though Catherine Flannagan evaded police for a time, both sisters were eventually caught and convicted of one of the murders; accordingly, they do not qualify as serial killers. They were both hanged on the same day in 1884 at Kirkdale Prison.	No	1	1+
27.	Steven John Grieveson (also known as "The Sunderland Strangler") murdered three teenage boys in the city of Sunderland, Tyne and Wear between 1993 and 1994 in order to conceal his homosexuality. He was convicted on 28 February 1996 and ordered to serve at least 35 years for the three murders. Three convictions for Murder do not qualify Grieveson as a serial killer.	No	3	3
28.	Stephen Griffiths (also known as the "Crossbow Cannibal") killed three female sex workers in the city of Bradford, West Yorkshire in 2009 and 2010. On 21 December 2010, Griffiths was convicted of all three murders and was sentenced to a whole life tariff. Three convictions for Murder do not qualify Griffiths as a serial killer.	No	3	3
29.	John George Haigh (also known as the "Acid Bath Murderer" and the "Vampire of London") was active in England during the 1940s. He was convicted of six murders, but claimed to have killed nine people. He used the acid baths not to kill his victims, but to dispose of their bodies, in the mistaken belief that he could not be convicted in the absence of the victim's body. He was executed at Wandsworth Prison in 1949. Six convictions qualify Haigh as a serial killer.	Yes	6	9
30.	Archibald Thomson Hall (a.k.a. Roy Fontaine) (also known as the "Monster Butler" and the "Killer Butler") was a thief and bisexual in 1977 and 1978 at a time when homosexuality was perceived as a problem. He was arrested after killing members of the British aristocracy in both England and Scotland in order to keep his secrets. Hall was convicted at courts in London and Edinburgh of four murders, with one left on file. At the time of his death, he was the oldest serving prisoner in a British prison. Four convictions for Murder do not qualify Hall as a serial killer.	No	4	5

No.	Details			
31.	Anthony Hardy (also known as the "Camden Ripper") was convicted of the murder and mutilation of three prostitutes. It is believed that Hardy may have committed as many as nine murders. He was sentenced to a whole life term, but does not qualify as a serial killer.	No	3	9
32.	Trevor Hardy (also known as "The Beast of Manchester") killed three teenage girls in Manchester between 1974 and 1976. He died after suffering a heart attack at Wakefield Prison. Three murders do not qualify him as a serial killer.	No	3	3
33.	Philip Herbert (also known as the "Infamous Earl of Pembroke") was a 17th century nobleman convicted of manslaughter but discharged. He later killed the prosecutor and received a pardon for a third murder. Never convicted of Murder, so not a serial killer.	No	0	3
34.	Colin Ireland (also known as the "Gay Slayer") killed five men from the Coleherne Public House, 261 Old Brompton Rd, Kensington, London SW5 in the early 1990s. These men were all homosexuals seeking partners for sado-masochistic activity. Ireland was gaoled for life for the murders in December 1993 and remained imprisoned until his death in February 2012, at the age of 57. His conviction for five Murders qualified Ireland as a serial killer.	Yes	5	5
35.	Kieran Patrick Kelly was a member of the South West London vagrant community, between frequent spells of imprisonment. When arrested on Clapham Common and taken to Clapham Police Station in 1983 he murdered a cellmate. When interviewed by Police he admitted fifteen more murders between 1953 and 1983 by pushing people that he had never met under London Underground trains. In 1984 at the Old Bailey he was convicted of one charge of Murder and one of Manslaughter; the other matters were left on file.	No	2	16
36.	Robin Ligus was a mental patient and drug addict convicted of robbing and bludgeoning three men to death with an iron bar in Shropshire in 1994. He was declared unfit to plead and detained indefinitely in a mental hospital. With no convictions, Ligus does not qualify as a serial killer.	No	0	3
37.	Michael Lupo (also known as "Wolf Man") claimed to be an active homosexual with 4,000 lovers, and that when he found that he was HIV positive he responded by killing four men. He was convicted of four murders and two attempted murders in 1986 and died in Durham Prison of an AIDs related condition in 1995. With just four convictions for Murder, Lupo cannot be classified as a serial killer.	No	4	4

No.	Facts	Serial Killer?	Convicted?	Suspected?
38.	Patrick Mackay (also known as "The Psychopath" and "The Devil's Disciple") became obsessed with Nazism. His mother arranged for him to be befriended by a Catholic priest, but Mackay stole £30 from him and then killed him with an axe. He then robbed and murdered a number of women. He was charged with the murders of five individuals, convicted of three, but admitted to killing eleven people. In November 1975 he was convicted of Manslaughter (due to diminished responsibility) and sentenced to Life Imprisonment and a whole life term. Three convictions for Manslaughter do not qualify Mackay as a serial killer.	No	3	11
39.	Peter Thomas Anthony Manuel (also known as "the Beast of Birkenshaw") was an American-born Scottish serial killer who was convicted of murdering seven people across Lanarkshire and southern Scotland between 1956 and his arrest in January 1958, and is believed to have murdered two more. He was hanged at Glasgow's Barlinnie Prison; he was one of the last prisoners to die on the Barlinnie gallows. He qualifies as a serial killer.	Yes	7	9
40.	Robert Maudsley, also known as "Hannibal the Cannibal"; garrotted a man who picked him up for sex in 1973, after the man showed him pictures of children that he had sexually abused. Maudsley was arrested, sentenced to a whole life term, and sent to Broadmoor Hospital. In 1977, Maudsley and another inmate took a third patient, a convicted child molester, hostage and locked themselves in a cell, before slowly torturing him to death. After this incident, Maudsley was convicted of manslaughter and sent to Wakefield Prison. He resented the transfer and pressed to return to Broadmoor. One afternoon in 1978 Maudsley killed two more fellow prisoners. Maudsley invited the first prisoner to his cell, where he garrotted and stabbed him before hiding his body. He then attempted to lure other prisoners into his cell, but all refused. Maudsley then went on the prowl around the wing hunting for a second victim, eventually cornering and stabbing and killing a second prisoner. Maudsley then calmly walked into the prison officer's room, placed the dagger on the table and told him that the next roll call would be two short. With one conviction for Murder and one for Manslaughter, Maudsley does not qualify as a serial killer.	No	2	4

No.	Description			
41.	Peter Moore (also known as "The man in black") is a Welshman, who between September and December 1995 stabbed to death and mutilated four homosexual men "for fun". He was sentenced to Life Imprisonment in November 1996. He does not qualify as a serial killer.	No	4	4
42.	Raymond Leslie Morris (also known as the "A34 Killer") was a Staffordshire paedophile who sexually abused and murdered girls aged between 5 and 9 years of age. He was convicted of one murder, but is strongly suspected of having committed at least two more. On 16 November 1968, Morris was found guilty of the rape and murder of 7-year-old Christine Darby and sentenced to Life Imprisonment. He died at HMP Preston on 11 March 2014, aged 84, having spent the final 45 years of his life in prison. He does not qualify as a serial killer, with only one conviction for Murder.	No	1	3+
43.	Robert Clive Napper (also known as "The Green Chain Rapist" and "The Plumstead Ripper") sexually attacked and murdered two young women in the presence of their young children, also killing one of the children, the murder of Rachel Nickell on Wimbledon Common in 1992 receiving considerable publicity. He was convicted of two murders and one of manslaughter (on the grounds of diminished responsibility, due to his mental health problems). He was remanded to Broadmoor Hospital indefinitely on 18 December 2008, but cannot be classified as a serial killer.	No	3	3
44.	Donald Neilson (b Donald Nappey) (also known as the "Black Panther") was an armed robber who murdered four people. Following three murders committed during robberies of sub-post offices from 1971 to 1974, he moved to kidnapping and made Lesley Whittle, an heiress from Highley, Shropshire, his first victim in early 1975, hiding her in underground drainage channels in Tamworth, Staffordshire. He was arrested later that year and sentenced to Life Imprisonment in 1976, remaining in prison until his death 35 years later. His four convictions for Murder do not qualify him as a serial killer.	No	4	4

No.	Facts	Serial Killer?	Convicted?	Suspected?
45.	Dennis Andrew Nilsen (also known as the "Muswell Hill Murderer" and the "Kindly Killer") is a homosexual and necrophiliac who was convicted of six murders and two attempted murders. He lured young homosexual men to one of two addresses that he occupied, through guile, and then murdered them by strangulation, sometimes accompanied by drowning. Following the murder, Nilsen would observe a ritual in which he bathed and dressed the victims' bodies, which he would retain for extended periods of time, before dissecting and disposing of the remains via burning upon a bonfire, or flushing the remains down a lavatory. In all, he is suspected of having committed sixteen murders. Nilsen was convicted of six murders and two attempted murders and on 4 November 1983 he was sentenced to Life Imprisonment. He qualifies as a serial killer.	Yes	6	16
46.	Colin Campbell Norris murdered four patients, all in their 80s, in Leeds General Infirmary and St James's Hospital in Leeds, in 2002. In the course of their investigation, the police looked into a total of 72 deaths. On 3 March 2008 Norris was convicted, by a majority verdict, of the murder of four women, and the attempted murder of a fifth. He was sentenced to Life Imprisonment, and ordered to serve a minimum term of 30 years. He does not qualify as a serial killer.	No	4	72
47.	Dr William Palmer (also known as the "Rugeley Poisoner" or the "Prince of Poisoners") was an English doctor who was convicted for the 1855 murder of his friend John Cook, and was executed in public by hanging the following year. He had poisoned Cook with strychnine, and was suspected of poisoning several other people including his mother-in-law, as well as four of his children who died of "convulsions" before their first birthdays. Palmer made large sums of money from the deaths of his wife and brother after collecting on life insurance, and by defrauding his wealthy mother out of thousands of pounds, all of which he lost through gambling on horses. Palmer does not meet the criteria for definition as a serial killer.	No	1	7

No.	Description			
48.	Dr Edward William Pritchard was an English doctor, living in Glasgow, who was convicted of murdering his wife and mother-in-law by poisoning. He was also suspected of a third murder, of a servant, but was never tried for it. Two years earlier their maid had died in a mysterious fire. He was the last person to be publicly executed in Glasgow in 1865. Pritchard cannot be defined as a serial killer.	No	2	3
49.	Harold Fredrick Shipman (also known as "Dr Death" and "The Angel of Death") was a British doctor and one of the most prolific serial killers in recorded history by proven murders. In July 2002, *The Shipman Inquiry* concluded that he had killed at least 215 of his patients (about 80% of whom were women) between 1975 and 1998, during which time he practiced as a general practitioner in Todmorden, West Yorkshire (1974–1975), and Hyde, Greater Manchester (1977–1998). On 31 January 2000, a jury found Shipman guilty of 15 specimen charges of murder. He was sentenced to Life Imprisonment and the judge recommended that he never be released. This made Shipman the only British doctor who has been found guilty of murdering his patients. On 13 January 2004, on the eve of his 58th birthday, Shipman hanged himself in his cell at Wakefield Prison. Subsequent enquiries have suggested that he may ultimately have been responsible for the deaths of as many as 457 of his patients. As a result of his conviction, the entire procedure surrounding the reporting and recording of death in the UK has been reviewed, and, where necessary revised. Shipman meets the requirements to be classified as a serial killer.	Yes	15	457
50.	George Joseph Smith (also known as "The Brides in the Bath Murderer") travelled around the country, seeking out women with savings, marrying them, insuring them and then murdering them. He developed a technique of surprising the women whilst they were bathing, by pulling their feet until their head slipped under the water and they drowned. He was convicted of the murder of three of his wives at the Old Bailey and hanged at Maidstone Prison on 13 August 1915. He does not meet the criteria for a serial killer.	No	3	3

No.	Facts	Serial Killer?	Convicted?	Suspected?
51.	John Straffen killed two girls, aged 5 and 9, in Bath in July and August 1951 "in order to annoy the police" whom he hated. He was found to be unfit to plead and was sent to Broadmoor Hospital. In April 1952 he escaped from Broadmoor and within a couple of hours had murdered another 5-year-old girl. This time he was convicted and sentenced to death. The Home Secretary commuted the sentence to Life imprisonment. Straffen died at Frankland Prison in County Durham on 19 November 2007 at the age of 77, when he had been in prison for a British record of 55 years. With one conviction, Straffen does not qualify as a serial killer.	No	1	3
52.	Peter William Sutcliffe (aka Peter William Coonan, also known as "The Yorkshire Ripper") was convicted of murdering and butchering thirteen women and attempting to murder seven others, between 1976 and 1981. His obsession with killing female street-based sex workers seems to have originated with an argument over payment, but he later claimed to have been sent on a mission to kill sex workers by the voice of God. When arrested in January 1981, for driving with false number-plates, police questioned him about the killings and he confessed that he was the perpetrator. Although at his trial he pleaded not guilty to murder on grounds of diminished responsibility, owing to a diagnosis of paranoid schizophrenia, this defence was rejected by a majority of the jury. He is serving twenty concurrent sentences of Life Imprisonment, currently in Broadmoor High Security Hospital. The High Court dismissed an appeal by Sutcliffe in 2010, confirming that he would serve a whole life tariff and would never be released from prison. Sutcliffe qualifies to be defined as a serial killer.	Yes	13	
53.	Peter Tobin was sentenced to ten years imprisonment for a double rape committed in 1993, and was released in 2004. In 2007, he was sentenced to life with a minimum of 21 years for a rape and murder in Glasgow in 2006. Skeletal remains of a further two young women who went missing in 1991 were subsequently found at his former home in Margate, Kent. Tobin was convicted of these murders in December 2008 and December 2009, and his minimum sentence was increased to 30 years. Tobin cannot be classified as a serial killer.	No	3	3+

#	Description			
54.	Thomas Griffiths Wainewright was an artist, author, and dandy with extravagant habits. In 1830 he insured the life of his sister-in-law, Helen Abercrombie, for a sum of £18,000, and when she died a few months later, payment was refused on the grounds of misrepresentation. Wainewright retired to Boulogne where he was found to be in possession of a quantity of strychnine and it was widely suspected that he had poisoned not only his sister-in-law and his uncle, but also his mother-in-law and a Norfolk friend, although this was never proved. He returned to London in 1837 but was at once arrested on a charge of forgery which had taken place thirteen years earlier, and transported to Australia. He died of apoplexy in the Hobart Town hospital on 17 August 1847. With no convictions for Murder, he cannot be classified as a serial killer.	No	0	4
55.	Margaret Waters was a baby-farmer; that is, one who took in other women's children for money, a practice often resulting in infanticide. She drugged and starved the infants in her care and is believed to have killed at least nineteen children. She was charged with five counts of murder as well as neglect and conspiracy, but was convicted of murdering just one infant, named John Walter Cowen. She was hanged at Horsemonger Lane Gaol (also known as Surrey County Gaol) on 11 October 1870. Having been convicted of just one Murder, Waters cannot be considered to be a serial killer.	No	1	19
56 and	Frederick Walter Stephen West and Rosemary West (also known as "House of Horrors" murderers) lived together at 25 Midland Road and later at 25 Cromwell Street, Gloucester.	Rose yes Fred no	Rose 10 Fred 0	
57.	Between 1967 and 1987, but mainly between May 1973 and August 1979, they tortured and raped many young women and girls, murdering at least eleven of them, including their own family members. The crimes often occurred in the couple's homes in the city of Gloucester, with many bodies buried at or near these homes. The pair were finally apprehended and charged in 1994. Fred West committed suicide before going to trial, while Rose West was jailed for life, in November 1995, after having been found guilty on 10 counts of murder. Their house at Cromwell Street was demolished in 1996 and the space converted into a landscaped footpath, connecting Cromwell Street to St. Michael's Square. Using the standard definition, Frederick West cannot be defined as a serial killer, but Rosemary West can be.	Both no		10+

No.	Facts	Serial Killer?	Convicted?	Suspected?
58.	Catherine Wilson worked as a nurse in Spalding, Lincolnshire, before moving to Kirkby, Cumbria. She poisoned her victims after encouraging them to leave her money in their wills. She was hanged for one murder, but was generally thought at the time to have committed six others. Wilson cannot be defined as a serial killer.	No	1	7
59.	Mary Elizabeth Wilson (née Cassidy) (also known as the "Merry Widow of Windy Nook"), married and lost four husbands between 1914 and 1957. Her "luck" was the subject of some debate locally, but it was her own sense of humour that led to her downfall. She joked at her last wedding reception that the leftover sandwiches would be fresh enough to use in the next funeral. She had also asked for a trade discount from the local undertaker, for providing him with plenty of business. These instances of morbid humour brought her to the attention of the police. When her fourth husband died she did not even bother to attend the funeral. When the bodies were exhumed, beetle poison was found to be the cause of the deaths of her first two husbands and phosphorous the cause of the deaths of her last two husbands. At Leeds Crown Court she was convicted of murdering her first two husbands and sentenced to death. It was thought unnecessary to charge her with the murder of her other two husbands. In view of her age (64 years) the sentence was commuted to Life Imprisonment. She died in Holloway Prison in 1963. Wilson does not qualify as a serial killer.	No	2	4
60.	Steven Gerald James Wright (also known as "The Suffolk Strangler") murdered five prostitutes all over Ipswich between 30 October and 10 December 2006. Their bodies were discovered naked, but there were no signs of sexual assault. Wright appeared at Ipswich Crown Court and pleaded not guilty to the charges, although he admitted having sex with all five victims, and that he had been patronising prostitutes since the 1980s. On 22 February 2008 Wright was convicted of all five murders and sentenced to a whole life term. Wright is a serial killer.	Yes	5	5

61.   Graham Frederick Young (also known as the "Teacup Poisoner") was sent to Broadmoor Hospital   No   0   3
in 1962 after poisoning several members of his family and killing his stepmother. Despite
spending his time at the hospital in the library studying poisons and managing to murder another
inmate with poison, Dr Edgar Udwin advised the Home Secretary that he had been cured and
could be safely released. Unfortunately, Young had not been cured and following his release in
1971 he went on to poison seventy more people, two of whom died. Young, was then sent to
Parkhurst Prison where he died of natural causes in 1990. Young does not meet the criteria to be
classified as a serial killer.

CHAPTER 2

The Coronation of Queen Elizabeth II

On 2 June 1953 Queen Elizabeth II of the United Kingdom, Canada, Australia, New Zealand, South Africa, Ceylon and Pakistan was crowned in Westminster Abbey. Approximately eight thousand VIP guests received personal invitations and attended the ceremony. Around three million people lined the route and several million more people from all over the world purchased television sets in order to watch the world's first major televised event.

Clearly, the event secured the succession of a Queen who, at that time, ruled over about a third of the world's land surface. It would have introduced the new Queen to the world and led to meetings between the eight thousand VIPs in attendance, who made up most of the Heads of State as well as just about all of the other 'movers and shakers' from around the world.

A less predictable consequence of the event, that had not been foreseen in the sixteen months of planning led by Prince Philip, the Duke of Edinburgh, that preceded it, was that a small, scruffy, drunken Irish vagrant from just outside Dublin came to London for a party, and while he was in London got a taste for killing people that stayed with him for thirty years and which led to him killing one person every day that he was not in prison for those thirty years. He did not know most of his victims and had no hatred of them; he just enjoyed killing people.

It is interesting to note that Ireland, both Northern Ireland and the Republic, have no record of ever having had a serial killer. Doctor Clements may have come close, but only committed four killings at the most, and was not convicted of any. Could it be that Ireland did what it does in so many areas, in that it exported its only serial killer?

Kieran Patrick Kelly came to London for the first time in his life ten days before the Coronation with a close friend from the same village just outside Dublin. The two men had served together in the Irish Army a little over a decade earlier and had developed an interest in partying. They enjoyed a good drink together and had learned how to survive in a big city.

Kelly was male, white, 5'4" tall, slim and wiry, with a very large, distinctive Roman nose, that caused most people to know him simply as 'Nosey'. He had just celebrated his 30th birthday and was currently unemployed and looking for work. His search was not helped by the fact that he drank heavily and frequently slept rough when he had drunk too much. He was generally scruffy. Most people passed him without a second look and told their children to look away from him, so as to avoid the possibility of his abusing them or assaulting them.

The two men had decided to move outside the big city with its expensive hotels in their search for a place to stay for their two-week stay in London, covering the build up to the Coronation, the event itself, and the days that followed the event. They had decided instead to move down one of the train lines belonging to London Underground and into the suburbs where they could live cheaply and travel up to London on the Underground every evening to party. Before coming to London, the two men had been told by friends who had worked as labourers there that the Northern Line was suitable for their purpose and that they could quickly and easily travel a few stops down the line to Clapham and Tooting in order to access cheap accommodation.

Upon their arrival in London, Kelly and his friend made their way to Tooting and went to the local pub, where they found a fellow Irishman who lived and worked in the town. Over a drink it was agreed that the two men could move in with their countryman for two weeks until just after the Coronation in exchange for a few quid.

Every night the two men went "up west" to the bright lights of Soho, drinking and partying. Kelly liked his drink and each night he enjoyed his fill, but it was starting to take its toll. A couple of days before the Coronation, the two men were at Tooting Broadway Underground Station, on the Northern Line northbound platform, chatting together and waiting for a train to take them up to Central London. Suddenly, and without warning, and for no apparent reason, his friend casually asked Kelly why it was that, at thirty years of age, Kelly was not married. It was an innocent question and was asked for no apparent reason, but it was to have disastrous consequences.

Kelly went silent. He tried to make light of the question and tried to pass it off by explaining that it was because he had not yet found the right woman. One day he would find that woman and they would settle down and have children. His friend, recognising that he had embarrassed Kelly with his question, tried to make a joke of it by suggesting that Kelly did not like girls. Nothing more was said and the matter was quickly forgotten as they continued their journey to Soho.

At the end of the evening the two men found two working girls, who had celebrated as well as they had, and when business had been transacted the girls agreed to go home with the guys for the night. The foursome managed to get themselves down to the London Underground, changing at Stockwell just in time for the last southbound train on the Northern Line.

They were enjoying what remained of the night. Kelly's friend had completely forgotten his earlier comments to Kelly, as they all laughed and joked together. But Kelly was in turmoil; he had not forgotten the comments; they had hurt him deeply. As the train arrived at the platform, Kelly saw what he later described as a blinding light, and he exploded. In front of the two girls and a substantial number of other passengers, he pushed his best friend underneath the tube train.

The two prostitutes panicked and ran out of the station. They knew that the police would have a low opinion of them and that they could expect to spend the next couple of days at the local police station answering questions about what the two men looked like, what they knew about their backgrounds, how they had met them, where they were going at the time of the incident, etc., etc., etc. It all sounded very unattractive, so off they went. There were no CCTV cameras in those days, and the girls were never seen again or identified. They are probably old age pensioners now, living with their secrets and never giving a thought to the incident at Stockwell and how it ended up.

The other passengers reacted in a similar manner. Some had been out partying with friends. They had probably had too much to drink; some may have been in possession of controlled drugs, or an offensive weapon; some may have had a history with the police, or been currently wanted in connection with a recent crime or traffic matter; some would have had a partner with them and been on a promise of favours to come when they arrived home. Why should they want to hang around to talk to the police? They did not know the man who had been killed. It was probably only an accident anyway. If they didn't talk to the Police, surely someone else would?

By the time that the British Transport Police (BTP), who were stationed in the office above Stockwell Underground Station but who were out and about on routine patrol at the time of the incident, arrived, there would have been a body under the train, a distraught train driver being comforted by his colleagues (many train drivers involved in hitting a pedestrian are so badly affected by the experience that they never drive a train again), and a London Ambulance Service crew waiting for permission to remove the body of the deceased, and not much else. Everybody else would have run off – and there was no CCTV. A quick look around, a search of the victim's pockets to identify him, a report to the CID and Police Duty Officer, and then inform the relatives and send the body off to hospital where death would be certified and wait for a call in due course with the date of the inquest.

Meanwhile, Kelly ran out of the station, constantly looking over his shoulder. He would not think that he could murder his pal and get away with it. He fully expected to be arrested in a minute or two and then, after a quick trial at the Old Bailey, taken away and hanged. That's what happened to murderers in 1953. It would be another twelve years before the death penalty was abolished for Murder under English Law.

If he was lucky he would get to spend the rest of his life in prison.

Kelly's mind was in turmoil as he struggled to come to terms with what he had done and what the consequences of his actions would be. Every police car that he saw, every policeman walking down the road, was chasing him, or so he thought. Every blue light or bell (police cars did not have two tones until 1965) that passed was searching for him. What should he do? Where should he go? Who could help him?

He knew that, barring miracles, his friend was dead. You don't get hit by a train at speed and survive. Who had seen what had happened? Did the two girls know his name? What had his friend told the girls about the two of them? What did the Police have to go on, because they would surely be involved?

Kelly struggled to understand what had happened that night. What had made him act in the way that he had done? Why had he killed his best friend? They had been friends for years. It didn't make sense to him at all. He was troubled by the way that he felt. He had enjoyed the kill. It had been exciting. Thrilling. He even got an erection from it. How did that work?

As time passed, Kelly slowly began to calm down, to come to terms with what happened and with what needed to be done. He still expected to be arrested eventually, but started to believe that it might take time to track him down.

Kelly decided to walk back to the room that they had been sharing in Tooting Broadway and keep his head down for a week or two. It was only about four miles and it gave him a chance to clear his head and to try to understand what had happened and why he had done what he had done. His mind raced as he tried to make sense of what had happened and what the future held for him.

It took him a little over an hour and a half to make it back to the room. He had drunk enough so that he quickly fell asleep. In the morning he woke early, and every time somebody walked past the house or rang the doorbell, he jumped, convinced that his time was up and that he was going to be dragged off to the local police station.

But the knock never came and Kelly just hid in the room. His landlord could not understand why he never left the room, even to buy food or drink. And what had happened to his mate? Why has he not come back after their night out? The landlord told him not to expect a refund just because his mate had gone off with some bird that he had picked up in London, or whatever. But Kelly had other worries and nothing was further from his mind than a refund for his absent friend.

Trapped in the flat for fear of being arrested, and with no alcohol, the pressure really got to Kelly as he struggled with his situation. He stopped bathing, washing or shaving, and his landlord lost patience with him. Eventually, Kelly packed his few belongings into his kitbag and decided to quickly head back to Dublin and keep his head down. He never did see the Coronation.

For the next six months in Dublin, Kelly lay low. He constantly worried that one day there would be a knock on the door and that when he went to the door there would be a group of Garda officers, accompanied by one of their colleagues from Scotland Yard, waiting to take him back to London to answer charges for what he had done.

But nothing happened and, bit by bit, Kelly got his confidence back and got back into the swing of things. After a year, when he had still heard nothing, he decided to return to London to seek the work that was escaping him in Dublin.

For the next thirty years, Kelly lived in fear of being found out, of being arrested and, until 1965, of being taken off and hanged. For the next couple of years, he lived quietly in London, found work and made a little money. He found a girl and they got married, settled down, and had a couple of children. Life was good. But Kelly never found peace, he could not forget about that night just before the Coronation, and what he had done to his best friend. He kept seeing flashbacks of the incident.

Life as a labourer in a big city has its ups and downs. When times are good, there is always plenty of work and plenty of money, but when recession hits, the jobs go and it is difficult to make money. This puts strain on a marriage and Kelly's was no different. His wife put pressure on Kelly to make money to feed the family.

When things went wrong and work was hard to come by, Kelly tried everything that he knew to make money. A little bit of theft here; a burglary there; a mugging when the opportunity arose. He dealt with the stress that he felt in the only way that he knew; he drank too much. It helped him to forget.

Eventually the inevitable happened: Kelly was arrested for Drunkenness. He knew what that meant. He would have to give his name and address. His fingerprints would be taken. The police would check their files, realise that he was the murderer from Stockwell Underground Station, he would be charged and finish up at the Old Bailey and being hanged.

When the next morning he appeared at South Western Magistrates Court in Lavender Hill in Battersea and was fined and released, Kelly became confused. Perhaps the police had not identified him as the murderer from Stockwell and he would not be hanged?

This was where things really went wrong for Kelly. He celebrated his release by drinking on Clapham Common with his friends, and when the drink ran out, it was Kelly who volunteered to go to the local shop and steal a few cans of drink, and it was he who was arrested. This time he was sent to prison for 9 months. It was the first of many such convictions and such sentences. Over the next thirty years Kelly would be sentenced to 3 years imprisonment, have a day out and then get sentenced to another 3 years. He was never out of prison for more than one or two days before being sent back in again.

Kelly quickly became a "face" around the prisons that surround Central London, Brixton, Wandsworth, Pentonville, and Wormwood Scrubs. On his days out he met the same people that he knew from prison on Clapham Common, Kennington Park, Tooting Bec, Camberwell Green, Wandsworth Common and so on.

Living with the same people in an 8-foot square prison cell or huddled together for warmth in a park or on commonland, means that they know all about each other's lifestyles, their backgrounds and history and that nobody has any secrets. Although nobody informed the police of Kelly's background, it does appear that it was general knowledge among his friends both in prison and in the parks and commonland that Kelly had killed and that he would probably do so again.

CHAPTER 3

The South West London

S outh West London is a smart and prosperous part of England. Bankers, business men and women, academics, doctors, dentists and industrialists drive their Mercedes, BMWs and Audi motor cars up and down the M3, M4, A3 and A4 roads that join London with Wales and the South West. They drive their smart cars to Heathrow and Gatwick Airports to make trips around the world for business and pleasure. They enjoy smart restaurants and public houses, usually belonging to the local Fuller's and Young's breweries and draw their children's attention to the dray horses delivering their beer to local hostelries.

The region is populated with large areas of park and common land, such as Burgess Park, Bushey Park, Camberwell Green, Clapham Common, Kennington Park, Kew Gardens, Mitcham Common, Morden Park, Richmond Park, Streatham Common, Tooting Bec, Wandsworth Common, Wimbledon Common, and Wimbledon Park.

Whilst these areas enjoy some exceptional facilities for sport and leisure, such as public meetings, pop concerts, horse riding, ice skating, rowing, canoeing and yachting, they are also frequented by large numbers of vagrants, who use them to drink and use drugs, as well as for sex and fighting.

It was into this area that in 1926, London Transport drove the southern extension of the Northern Line of the London Underground, restructured Kennington and Kennington Oval Stations and then built new stations at Stockwell, Clapham North, Clapham Common, Clapham South, Balham, Tooting Broadway, Tooting Bec, South Wimbledon, Colliers Wood and Morden. The Northern Line had an immediate and, some would say, devastating effect on the area, massively expanded the population, and filling the area with new houses, new businesses and new workers, which it took into Central London every day in order to maintain the economy of the city.

For over sixty years, from its construction in 1926 until the implementation of the Fennell Review that followed the Kings Cross Fire that occurred on 18 November 1987, access to the underground stations across the network was unrestricted and members of the public just wandered in and out of stations, past ticket offices and latterly ticket machines, buying tickets as they thought fit. There was little enforcement of the requirement to possess a ticket for the journey before entering the station.

Prior to 1987 there was little control of the access and egress from London Underground Stations. Regular financial cutbacks had drastically reduced the number of staff throughout the long days during which Underground Stations are open. Any bold ticket collector who challenged somebody for entering a station or travelling without a ticket was likely to very quickly become a victim of violence and would not have the support that he or she required to enforce the decision.

Only after the Kings Cross Fire was the danger associated to allowing free access to the Underground network recognised and ticket machines fitted to every entrance and exit of every station. Suddenly the number of people visiting Underground Stations and travelling on trains were reduced and the London Underground network became a far more pleasant and far safer place to be.

Policing the London Undergound

Responsibility for policing the London Underground rests with the British Transport Police, a small force of officers with responsibilities across the four Home Countries of England, Wales, Scotland and Northern Ireland, across different legal jurisdictions, across all Force boundaries, and funded, according to a complex formula, by the train and bus companies rather than the Home Office like the territorial Forces.

The funding arrangements that the Chief Constable has, means that he has to have one eye on who has paid their bill recently before allocating his officers to their various duties. It is a sensitive situation and not a task that I envy him. In recent years the Metropolitan Police have recognised these issues and the problems that they create by agreeing with the British

Transport Police for their officers to travel on the Underground and on local buses.

Knowing that Police officers are working in the area makes station staff more confident of being able to challenge those who enter the station, or travel on trains, without the necessary authority to do so. It makes for a safer and more attractive railway, where the likes of Kieran Patrick Kelly are more likely to be looking over their shoulder than the station staff.

To put the story of Kieran Patrick Kelly into context, it would help to understand the area.

Morden

Morden is situated approximately 10 miles/18 km south-southwest of Central London, between Merton Park (to the north), Mitcham (to the east), Sutton (to the south) and Worcester Park (to the west). The name derives from the Celtic *Mawr* (great or large) and *Dun* (a fort), or possibly "The Town on the Moor". Morden is a town in the London Borough of Merton.

Local industry was mainly agricultural in nature and it was not until 1926, when the City & South London Railway (now part of the London Underground's Northern Line) built its southern extension and Morden Underground Station opened as the terminus, that the fast and direct route to Central London opened the village to residential development.

Away from the new commercial centre of Morden, the existing rural roads were widened and rebuilt and the fields were rapidly divided into building plots and laid out for new housing. Further transport improvements came with the construction of a new Southern Railway branch line from Wimbledon to Sutton via stations at South Merton and Morden South (so named to differentiate it from Morden Underground Station and Morden Station (now Morden Road tram stop), although it was actually north east of the original village centre). The new line opened in January 1930.

As a result of the new transport links, the population of Morden increased rapidly from 1,355 in 1921 to 12,618 in 1931. In the next fifteen years, the population continued to grow, as most of the parish was covered in new suburban homes.

Population of Morden

19th century		20th century	
1801	512	1901	960
1811	549	1911	1,202
1821	638	1921	1,355
1831	655	1931	12,618
1841	685	1941	WWII
1851	628	1951	35,417
1861	654	1961	68,011
1871	787	1971	62,872
1881	694	1981	61,108
1891	763	1991	N/A

South Wimbledon

South Wimbledon (formerly New Wimbledon) is an area in the London Borough of Merton in south west London. It is situated approximately 8 miles/13 km south-southwest of Central London, between Tooting (to the north), Mitcham (to the east), Morden (to the south) and Wimbledon (to the west).

Colliers Wood

Colliers Wood is an area in south west London, in the London Borough of Merton. It is situated approximately 7 miles/12 km south-southwest of Central London, between Tooting (to the north), Streatham (to the east), Morden (to the south) and Wimbledon (to the west).

The town takes its name from a wood that stood to the east of the present High Street, approximately where Warren, Marlborough and Birdhurst Roads are currently situated. It was finally cleared between 1870 and 1895.

Colliers Wood is home to the twelfth century ruin at Merton Priory, one of the places in the UK considered by the Department of Culture, Media and Sport to go forward as a British candidate for World Heritage status. Henry VI, the only king of England not to be crowned in Westminster Abbey in the last 1,000 years, held his coronation ceremony at Merton Priory in 1437. Among those educated at the priory were Thomas Becket and Nicholas Breakspear, who was the only English Pope.

Close to Merton Priory is the market and heritage centre at Merton Abbey Mills, which is on the bank of the River Wandle. The Wandle was reputed to have more mills per mile than any other river in the world, ninety mills along its eleven mile length. William Morris, at the forefront of the Arts and Crafts Movement, relocated his dyeworks to Merton Abbey Mills, after determining that the water of the Wandle was suitable for dyeing. The complex, on 7 acres, included several buildings and a dyeworks, and the various buildings were soon adapted for stained-glass, textile printing, and fabric- and carpet-weaving. The works closed in 1940. The site is now occupied by a large shared Sainsbury/M&S supermarket complex.

The world's first public railway, the Surrey Iron Railway, passed through Colliers Wood on its route from Croydon to Wandsworth, between 1803 and 1846.

Tooting

Tooting is a district in South London, located in the London Borough of Wandsworth. It is situated 5 miles/8 km south south-west of Charing Cross. The area is identified in the London Plan as one of 35 major centres in Greater London. It has been settled since pre-Saxon times.

The name 'Tooting' is of Anglo-Saxon origin but the meaning is disputed. It could mean *the people of Tota*, where Tota may have been a local Anglo-Saxon chieftain. Alternatively, it could be derived from an old meaning of the verb *to tout*, to look out. There may have been a watchtower here on the road to London and hence: *the people of the look-out post*.

The Romans built a road, which was later named Stane Street by the English, from London (Londinium) to Chichester (Noviomagus Reginorum), and which passed through Tooting. Tooting High Street is built on this road. In Saxon times, Tooting and Streatham (then Toting-cum-Stretham) was given to the Abbey of Chertsey. Later, Suene (Sweyn), believed to be a Viking, may have been given all or part of the land. In 933,

King Athelstan of England is thought to have confirmed lands including Totinge (Tooting) to Chertsey Abbey.

As with many of South London's suburbs, Tooting developed during the late Victorian period. Some development occurred in the Edwardian era but another large spurt in growth happened during the 1920s and '30s.

Tooting Bec

Tooting Bec is a town in the London Borough of Wandsworth in south London. It is situated approximately 6 miles/10 km south-southwest of Central London, between Battersea (to the north), Streatham (to the east), Mitcham (to the south) and Wimbledon (to the west).

It is named after Bec Abbey in Normandy, which was given land in this area (then part of the Streatham parish) after the Norman Conquest. Saint Anselm, the second Abbot of Bec, is reputed to have been a visitor to Tooting Bec long before he succeeded Lanfranc as Archbishop of Canterbury. Saint Anselm gives his name to the modern Roman Catholic Church which sits on the corner of Balham High Road and Tooting Bec Road. A relief sculpture of Saint Anselm visiting the Totinges tribe (from which Tooting as a whole gets its name) is visible on the exterior of Wandsworth Town Hall.

The Romans built a road, which was later named Stane Street by the English, from London (Londinium) to Chichester (Noviomagus Reginorum), and which passed through Tooting. Tooting Bec sits on Stane Street.

The area includes Tooting Common, which features Tooting Bec Lido, the largest fresh water pool in England as well as an athletics stadium. Often considered part of Tooting, it forms the northern part of the latter suburb.

Balham

Balham is a town in the London Borough of Wandsworth in south London. It is situated approximately 5 miles/10 km south-southwest of Central London, between Battersea (to the north), Streatham (to the east), Mitcham (to the south) and

Wandsworth (to the west). The town is situated between four south London commons: Clapham Common to the north, Wandsworth Common to the west, Tooting Graveney Common to the south, and the adjoining Tooting Bec Common to the east – the latter two historically distinct areas are referred to by both Wandsworth Council and some local people as Tooting Common. Other nearby areas include Tooting, Streatham, Brixton and Battersea.

The settlement appears in the *Domesday Book* as *Belgeham*. Bal refers to 'rounded enclosure' and ham to a homestead, village or river enclosure. Balham is recorded in several maps in the 1600s as Ballam or Balham Hill or Balham Manor.

On 14 October 1940 Balham tube station was involved in bombing raids which took place in London during the Second World War. People took cover in the tube station. A bomb landed directly on top of the station, bursting water and gas mains and killing sixty-four people.

The Bedford is a pub venue for live music and comedy on Bedford Hill; performers at the *Banana Cabaret* have included Eddie Izzard, Jo Brand and Al Murray. In 1876, the building (then named the "Bedford Hotel") housed the coroner's inquest into the notorious unsolved murder of Charles Bravo, a resident and lawyer who was poisoned, possibly by his wife.

The Bedford Hill area of Balham was associated with street prostitution throughout the 1970s and '80s. The problem has since been eradicated.

Clapham

Clapham is situated approximately 4 miles/7 km south-southwest of Central London, between Battersea (to the north and west), Streatham (to the south) and Brixton (to the east).

In the early twentieth century, Clapham was seen as an ordinary commuter suburb, often cited as representing ordinary people: hence the so-called "Man on the Clapham omnibus". By the 1980s the area had undergone a further transformation, becoming the centre for the gentrification of most of the surrounding area. Clapham's proximity to the traditionally upper-class areas of Sloane Square and Belgravia, which became increasingly unaffordable to all but the very wealthy in the boom years of the 1980s and 1990s, led to a colonisation of the area by the middle classes.

Today Clapham is an affluent multi-cultural neighbourhood, home to middle-class British professionals, overseas (Irish, African, Caribbean, South-American, European, Australian and North-American) residents, middle-class people of BME origin and a vibrant gay community. Many young university graduates and students also choose to live in the Clapham area, a tradition carried over from the days when some University of London halls of residence were situated there. Most recently, there has been a surge in the numbers of young, well-educated Irish settling in the area.

The present day Clapham High Street is an ancient "diversion" of the Roman military road Stane Street, which ran from London to Chichester. This followed the line of Clapham Road and then onward along the line of Abbeville Road. The ancient status of that military road is recorded on a Roman stone now placed by the entrance of Clapham Library in the Old Town, which was discovered during building operations at Clapham Common South Side in 1912. Erected by Vitus Ticinius Ascanius according to its inscription, it is estimated to date from the first century.

According to the 2001 census Clapham and Stockwell town centre had a joint population of 65,513 inhabitants.

Stockwell

Stockwell is a district in inner south London, located in the London Borough of Lambeth. It is situated 2.4 miles/3.9 km south south-east of Central London. Vauxhall (to the north,) Battersea (to the west), Clapham (to the south) and Brixton (to the east). Once one of London's poorest neighbourhoods, it is now an up-and-coming area, owing to its close proximity to Central London and excellent transport links.

Stockwell probably got the second half of its name from a local well; the other half is from "stoc", which was Old English for a tree trunk or post.

Its social and architectural fortunes in the twentieth century were more mixed. The area immediately around Stockwell tube station was extensively rebuilt following the Second World War, and the original domed tube station was replaced first in the 1920s, then again with the opening of the Victoria Line in 1971.

The area also has much social housing; the main estates are Lansdowne Green, Stockwell Park, Staley, Spurgeon, Morsel and Stockwell Gardens. However, many remnants of the area's nineteenth century grandeur can be found in the side and back streets of Stockwell, notably in the Stockwell Park Conservation Area, mostly built between 1825 and 1840 and centred on Stockwell Park Road.

Stockwell and neighbouring South Lambeth are home to one of the UK's biggest Portuguese communities, known as 'Little Portugal'. Most of the local Portuguese people originate from Madeira and Lisbon and have established many cafes, restaurants, bakeries, neighbourhood associations and delicatessens. Stockwell is also home to many people of Caribbean and West African origin. They are also well represented in the local population, and cafes, grocers, barbers' shops and salons run by people from these communities are scattered around Stockwell.

In 1986 Kenneth Erskine, a serial killer dubbed the Stockwell Strangler, killed seven elderly victims, three of whom were from Stockwell.

On 22 July 2005, following the 21 July 2005 London bombings, Stockwell gained notoriety as the scene of the shooting by police of an innocent Brazilian electrician, Jean Charles de Menezes, in the tube station.

Kennington

Kennington is situated approximately 2 miles/4 km south of Central London, between Waterloo (to the north), Walworth (to the east), Brixton (to the south) and Belgravia (to the west).

Kennington appears in the Domesday Book of 1086 as *Chenintune*. It is recorded as *Kenintone* in 1229 and *Kenyngton* in 1263. Mills (2001) believes the name to be Old English, meaning 'farmstead or estate associated with a man called Cēna'. Another explanation is that it means "place of the King", or "town of the King".

Kennington is a district situated in Central London south of the River Thames. It is mainly within the London Borough of Lambeth, although parts of the district fall within the London Borough of Southwark.

Kennington is the location of several significant London landmarks: the Oval cricket ground, the Imperial War Museum and Kennington Park. The population of Kennington at the United Kingdom Census 2011 was 21,287.

CHAPTER 4

The Parks and Common Land in South West London

South West London is particularly well provided for in terms of common and park land. Wide open spaces, such as Richmond Park, Wimbledon Common, Wimbledon Park, Clapham Common and Streatham Common allow children to learn about nature, to run wild without the risk of disturbing adults, to play games and to keep fit. They are a great gift and provide social, cultural and sporting facilities for the entire community. Unfortunately, they also attract unpleasant elements of the community such as alcoholics, drug offenders and even sexual predators, such as Robert Napper (featured earlier) who killed Rachel Nickell.

In these areas, Kieran Patrick (Nosey) Kelly was king. In this alternative society he met up with other like-minded individuals who had been shunned by polite, decent society and drank alcohol and took drugs in order to escape their sins and forget their pasts. Many of them came from Ireland, Scotland and Wales where unemployment had been high and social drinking was popular. Many had joined the Army, the Navy or the Air Force in order to escape their problems and find security, and then found that their alcoholism, drug taking and sexual predation had excluded them rather than included them.

The vagrants of the parks collect in groups in order to share each other's company and because on any one day, only one or two of them will have the money to buy drink or drugs; sharing becomes a way of life so that the group can secure the needs of the individual. The drink and drugs frequently lead them to fall asleep where they are, so the park becomes their home. They do not have washing or laundry facilities so very soon they start to smell. They are avoided by polite society, and they become grumpy and abusive.

Police officers quickly learn to avoid such groups. Offences of drunkenness, minor disorder, possession of drug paraphernalia, even assault where the victim is homeless and lost, will not gain anybody credit or promotion. Anyway, who wants to get up close and personal with unwashed people who have recently suffered with vomiting and diarrhoea? Best to walk the other way ...

When the Police abdicate their responsibilities, the only authority is the biggest bully in the gang. Kelly was physically insignificant, 5'4" tall, slim build, and weakened by drugs and alcohol, but "in the land of the blind, the one eyed man is king" and Kelly's compatriots were even more drunk and incapable than he was. He was able to exercise a firm control over those around him.

Nosey was very aware of his vulnerability. He knew that he was small, physically weak and frequently intoxicated and that he could easily be assaulted or even murdered by any one of his colleagues. He learned to use his mind to outwit his colleagues and to ruthlessly strike first if he felt threatened. He related a story to the author that on one occasion he overheard his friends talk of "grassing him to the Police", so he decided to buy them all a drink. Unfortunately for them, when he went to the corner store to buy them the drink, he purchased white spirit (a lethal paint stripper) rather than lager, cider or sherry. Those who did not die spent considerable periods in hospital and when they were released from hospital they could no longer remember what it was that they had been intending to report to the Police.

Kelly became quite proficient at shoplifting and walk-in theft. He supported himself by taking what he wanted and becoming abusive and violent when challenged by shopkeepers. Most of them learned that it was easier to let him take what he wanted than risk being assaulted or spending days writing statements and attending court to give evidence. Possession of food and drink also gave Nosey control over his compatriots. If they wanted to share his food and drink then they had to do as he told them. This, of course, extended to allowing him to satisfy his sexual urges.

There are fifteen large open spaces in South West London:

Burgess Park is a public park of 140 acres situated approximately 600 metres north of Camberwell Green. It was formed when, in the 1970s, all the Victorian housing and industrial premises situated between Walworth Road/Camberwell Road and the Old Kent Road were demolished to build the Heygate and Aylesbury Housing Estates.

As part of the clear-up operation in the 1980s the area between Camberwell Road, Albany Road, Old Kent Road, Trafalgar Avenue, St George's Way and New Church Road was formed into Burgess Park, in order to provide leisure and recreation facilities for those living in the new, high-intensity housing nearby.

While some of the housing that was demolished was in poor condition, many perfectly serviceable homes were demolished in order to build the new estates and the park. This has resulted in strong local feelings about the park. It has also generated allegations that the housing was demolished in order to remove the criminal fraternity, the infamous Richardson Gang (which dominated South London and tortured its rivals and was based in New Church Road) and the founders of the National Front (who held their first meetings in New Church Road).

The boundaries of Burgess Park remain a matter of dispute and several former roads have been closed but not yet grassed over so as to truly become part of the park. Considerable sums of money continue to be invested in the area by central government, the London Mayor and the local Southwark Council, in order to promote a range of new initiatives to maximise the usefulness of the area to the community.

Despite the area's proximity to Camberwell Green and its good transport links, its popularity with local residents and the lack of any local shops selling alcohol has meant that it has been almost totally ignored by the vagrant community.

Bushey Park (including Hampton Court Park) is the second largest of London's Royal Parks, at 1,100 acres in area. It is made up of three ancient parks, Hare Warren, Middle Park and Bushey Park and lies immediately north of Hampton Court Palace and Hampton Court Park. It is surrounded by Teddington, Hampton, Hampton Hill and Hampton Wick, and is a few minutes walk from the north side of Kingston Bridge.

The Longford River, a nineteen kilometre canal to provide water to Hampton Court, and the park's various ponds were built on the orders of Charles I. This period also saw the construction of the main thoroughfare, Chestnut Avenue, which runs from Park Road in Teddington to the Lion Gate entrance of Hampton Court Palace in Hampton Court Road. This avenue and the Arethusa 'Diana' Fountain were designed by Sir Christopher Wren as a grand approach to Hampton Court Palace.

Originally created for royal sports, Bushey Park is now home to Teddington Rugby Club, Teddington Hockey Club (from 1871 onwards, the rules of the modern game of field hockey were largely devised at Bushey), and four cricket clubs, including Teddington Town Cricket Club, Hampton Wick Royal Cricket Club, Teddington Cricket Club and Hampton Hill Cricket Club.

The park also contains several lodges and cottages, Bushy House, the National Physical Laboratory (NPL) at the Teddington end and the Royal Paddocks, and two areas of allotments: the Royal Paddocks Allotments at Hampton Wick and the Bushey Park Allotments at Hampton Hill.

As part of an upgrade of the park facilities, the new Pheasantry Café was added, and the restored and largely reconstructed Upper Lodge Water Gardens were opened in October 2009. Bushey Park is not a home to vagrants.

Camberwell Green is a small area of common land next to a major traffic intersection in South London. The A202 takes traffic travelling from the Continent and Kent from the A2 at New Cross, along Peckham Road and Camberwell Church Street, past Camberwell Green, and along Camberwell New Road and over Vauxhall Bridge to Victoria Station. The A215 takes traffic from South Norwood, along Herne Hill and Denmark Hill, past Camberwell Green to Camberwell Road and Walworth Road to the A3 at the Elephant and Castle roundabout.

The Green is surrounded by intense residential development to the north and intense commercial development on the other three sides. At the north-east corner of the Green is Camberwell Magistrates Court, and to the south west is a parade of shops which includes the office of a local solicitor and a large chemist shop.

This configuration means that every day the local Police deliver all those arrested for Drunkenness, Vagrancy, Disorder, Possession of Drugs and minor crime, across a swathe of South London that includes Deptford, Lewisham, Camberwell, Walworth, Brixton and Kennington to the court and that many of these people then remain in the area in order to instruct their solicitors and prepare for their forthcoming trials and to receive their daily allocations of prescribed drugs.

Camberwell Green is one mile south east of Oval Underground Station and one and a half miles south of the Elephant and Castle and Kennington Underground Stations, although there are regular, direct services from all these stations.

As a result of all these factors there are frequently between 50 and 100 vagrants on Camberwell Green at any one time, so they form an intimidating presence to ordinary members of the public. An attempt by local police to clear the common a few years ago resulted in a major confrontation, a substantial number of injuries to both sides and a new sign, painted by the vagrants, proclaiming that "Carter Street Old Bill Rule OK?" in two foot high letters.

Clapham Common is a triangular area of 220 acres of grassland situated within the London Borough of Wandsworth and the London Borough of Lambeth. It was historically common land for the parishes of Battersea and Clapham, but was converted to parkland under the terms of the Metropolitan Commons Act 1878.

The Common contains three ponds. Eagle Pond and Mount Pond are used for angling and contain a variety of species including carp, roach, tench and bream, while Long Pond has a century-old tradition of use for model boating. There is also a more modern paddling pool known as Cock Pond.

The common is surrounded by many fine houses, built from the 1790s onwards, which became fashionable dwellings for wealthy business people in what was then a village detached from metropolitan London. Some were members of the Clapham Sect of evangelical reformers, including Lord Teignmouth and Henry Thornton, the banker and abolitionist. As London expanded in the 19th century, Clapham was absorbed into the capital, with most of the remaining palatial or agricultural estates replaced with terraced housing by the early 1900s.

In the centre of the Common is the Clapham bandstand constructed in 1890. It is the largest bandstand in London and a Grade II Listed Building.

Former Welsh Secretary in the UK government Ron Davies had a "moment of madness" in 1998 in an incident that took place on the Common. He met some strangers on the Common to whom he gave a lift; those same people robbed him at knife point and took his car, wallet and phone. Davies resigned, repeatedly denying the incident had anything to do with drugs or sex. Newspapers have since reported that Mr Davies admits being bisexual and has "been successfully treated for a compulsion to seek out gay partners".

Kennington Park is a large area of parkland next to a major traffic intersection in South London. The A3 takes traffic from Portsmouth, along Clapham High Street, past Kennington Park and along Kennington Park Road to London Bridge. Nowadays Clapham Common is home to hundreds of vagrants.

With the park being just a mile from the Houses of Parliament and Whitehall, and with public protest and demonstration around Parliament restricted by statute, Kennington Park has a 500 year history as a venue for public speaking and public meetings, and as a place for people to meet up prior to public marches. Some of the most illustrious orators to speak in the park were the founders of the Methodist religion, George Whitefield (1714–70) and John Wesley (1703–91). They are reputed to have attracted crowds of 30,000 people.

On 10 April 1848, the Chartists gathered on Kennington Common for a 'monster rally', and it was soon after this, in 1854 that, sponsored by members of the Royal Family, the common was enclosed and converted into Kennington Park.

After the Napoleonic Wars, thousands of soldiers and sailors returned to find themselves penniless and homeless; they lived on the street and caused problems. In 1824 Parliament passed the Vagrancy Act and made living on the streets, after being directed to a hostel by a Policeman, an offence. The only hostel anywhere near London was Consort Road in Peckham and every vagrant had to walk towards it or face prosecution. Today, all the vagrants found in the Cities of London and Westminster are still directed to walk to Kennington Park and turn left into Camberwell New Road, along Peckham Road to Consort Road. It cannot be surprising that, particularly on hot, sunny days, many develop a strong thirst and feel the need to stop off at Kennington Park for a drink and a chat.

Situated so close to Central London, very close to two London Underground Stations and a host of London Transport buses, and the direct routes to Consort Road, it can be no surprise that the park is regularly occupied by up to a hundred vagrants.

During the Kelly Enquiry, the author was sent to Kennington Park for a couple of weeks to trace a witness and, in order to befriend the vagrants and secure the information that he required, he used his expenses to buy beer, lager, cider and sherry and became very popular with the local vagrants. The local vagrants are generally comparatively well behaved, as the park is close to residential areas and to busy roads so that any inappropriate behaviour is promptly reported to the Police.

Kew Gardens is occupied by the Royal Botanic Gardens, the world's largest collection of living plants. The organisation employs more than 650 scientists and other staff. The living collections include more than 30,000 different kinds of plants, while the herbarium, which is one of the largest in the world, has over seven million preserved plant specimens. The library contains more than 750,000 volumes, and the illustrations collection contains more than 175,000 prints and drawings of plants. The Kew site includes four Grade I listed buildings and 36 Grade II listed structures in an internationally significant landscape.

The constant visits to the site preclude its use by vagrants.

Mitcham Common is 460 acres of common land situated between Thornton Heath and Mitcham, on the borders of London and Surrey. The land has few natural advantages, is in poor condition and is generally used for gravel extraction for building purposes, so that large areas are covered in water. The common is two and a half miles from the nearest London

Underground Station and with poor London Transport bus connections. The area is generally overlooked by the vagrant community.

Morden Park is an area of parkland south of, and close to, Morden town centre. It covers land that previously formed the grounds of Morden Park House, a small eighteenth century country estate. Morden Park House remains and, after many years of neglect and semi-dereliction, has recently been restored and is now the local register office and a venue for wedding ceremonies. It should not to be confused with Morden Hall Park, the National Trust property on the other side of Morden town centre

The Park includes the land itself, an area of green space in an otherwise dense cluster of 1930s suburban housing. The present park and sports fields between Hillcross Avenue, London Road/ Epsom Road and Lower Morden Lane are owned and managed by the London Borough of Merton Parks Department.

The entrance to the Park, from London Road, is now dominated by the Merton Campus of South Thames College (formerly Merton College), built in the late 1960s. Facilities in Morden Park include a pitch and putt golf course and Morden Park Swimming Pool which was opened in 1967 on the site of the old house's gardens.

Morden is a quiet, suburban area without any vagrants and none are ever found in Morden Park.

Peckham Rye is an open space situated between Peckham and East Dulwich in South London. It is triangular in shape, located between two roads, both named simply Peckham Rye, and another road called Colyton Road, and consists of two congruent areas, with Peckham Rye Common to the north and Peckham Rye Park to the south.

The 54 acres of land on which Peckham Rye Park sits were purchased by the London County Council in 1894 for £51,000.

Peckham Rye is very close to the Homeless Centre in Consort Road and this draws a number of vagrants to the Rye, but the fact that it is three bus rides away from the nearest London Underground Station means that it is inaccessible to most vagrants.

Richmond Park is the second largest park in London (after Lee Valley Park) and is Britain's second largest urban walled park (after Sutton Park in Birmingham), measuring 3.69 square miles/2,360 acres. It is a National Nature Reserve, a Site of Special Scientific Interest and a Special Area of Conservation in south-west London. The largest of London's Royal Parks, it is included, at Grade I, on English Heritage's Register of Historic Parks and Gardens of special historic interest in England. It was created by Charles I in 1634 as a deer park and now has 630 red and fallow deer.

A mugging at gunpoint in 1854 reputedly led to the establishment of a park police force. Until 2005 the park was policed by the separate Royal Parks Constabulary but that has now been subsumed into the Royal Parks Operational Command Unit of the Metropolitan Police. In recent years the mounted police have been replaced by a patrol team in a four-wheel drive vehicle.

Being in a smart, suburban area and with its own private police force, these factors have kept vagrants out of Richmond Park.

Streatham Common is situated on the A23 London to Brighton road between two substantial shopping centres, in Streatham and Norbury. From Streatham High Road the land inclines gently upward towards West Norwood and as the land is clear, local residents overlook all areas of the common.

The Rookery car park at the far end of the common is surrounded by trees and has become an area of intense sexual activity during the hours of darkness. The lower edge of the common is close to Streatham Bus Garage, with excellent bus routes in all direction, so the common attracts a small number of vagrants, without ever attracting a crowd.

Tooting Bec is situated between Bedford Hill, Elmbourne Road, Tooting Bec Road and Garrards Road, just a little way behind Streatham High Road and between Streatham and Tooting in South London. The area has had a very bad reputation for street prostitution since the Second World War as a result of the US Army situating a barracks in Bedford Hill during the war.

Vagrants are seldom seen on Tooting Bec due to its distance from the London Underground and the fact that they would have to compete for space with the prostitutes.

Wandsworth Common is an area of common land 171 acres in area, and roughly bordered by Bolingbroke Grove, Trinity Road and Burntwood Lane. Wandsworth Common Railway Station is located at the junction of Bellevue Road, St James's Drive and Nightingale Lane and broadly divides the common into two strips. A footbridge crosses the railway approximately halfway along the length of the open part of the common.

The area around the common is occupied by large, older-type houses which have recently been restored and renovated. They are generally occupied by young professional couples who have pushed to have a wider range of facilities set up on the common. There are a large number of lakes and ponds on the common and these have been arranged to encourage bird life, interaction with nature and, with a permit, fishing. Nature walks, exercise trails and sports pitches have also been built. Other facilities include an educational centre in an area dedicated to wildlife known locally as 'The Scope' (named after the Craig telescope, which was once the largest refracting telescope in the world). There are also tennis courts, a bowling green and a cafe bar in the grounds, named 'Common Ground'. The Common is popular with local runners, dog walkers and cyclists.

The popularity of the common, its proximity to local housing and its open layout mean that there are other areas better suited to vagrants and that the common is generally vagrant-free.

Wimbledon Common is a large open space covering 1,100 acres. There are three named areas: Wimbledon Common, Putney Heath, and Putney Lower Common, which together are managed under the name Wimbledon and Putney Commons. Putney Lower Common is separated from the rest of the Common by about 1.5 miles of built-up area.

Wimbledon Common, together with Putney Heath and Putney Lower Common, is protected by the Wimbledon and Putney Commons Act of 1871 from being enclosed or built upon. The Common is for the benefit of the general public for informal recreation, and for the preservation of natural flora and fauna. It is the largest expanse of heathland in the London area. There is an area of bog with unique flora. The western slopes, which lie on London Clay, support mature mixed woodland. The Commons are also a flagship site for the stag beetle. Most of the area is a Site of Special Scientific Interest, and a Special Area of Conservation under the EC Habitats Directive.

The Commons are managed by the Clerk and Ranger, supported by a Deputy, a Wildlife & Conservation Officer and a personal assistant. There are seven Mounted Keepers (who deal with public safety and security), two groundsmen (for the playing fields), six maintenance workers and one property maintenance worker – some nineteen employees in total. There are at least four horses which are used by the Keepers on mounted patrol.

The Commons are administered by eight Conservators. The Conservators are responsible for the annual budget of around £1m. Most of the revenue comes from an annual levy on houses within $^3/_4$ mile of the Commons. The levy payers are entitled to vote for the five elected Conservators.

There is nothing like have ownership of property to make people take responsibility for an area. The local residents enforce high standards on the common and there are no vagrants to be found anywhere.

Wimbledon Park is the name of an urban park in Wimbledon and also of the suburb south and east of the park and the nearby London Underground station. The park itself is 67 acres in area. The All England Lawn Tennis and Croquet Club is immediately to the west of the park. Wimbledon Park should not be confused with the much larger and better known Wimbledon Common, further to the west up the hill.

The original park comprised part of the grounds of Wimbledon House, the seat of the manor of Wimbledon, situated on the hill to the south, near St Mary's Church, the old parish church of Wimbledon. A series of owners enlarged the park northwards and eastwards. By the 19th century it was at its largest extent, and one of the homes of the Earls Spencer, lords of the manor. The park had been landscaped in the 18th century by Capability

Brown when the lake was formed by constructing a dam across a brook that flows from the springline near Wimbledon Common down to the River Wandle in Earlsfield.

The modern park was purchased by the Borough of Wimbledon just before the First World War and is, with its ornamental lake, the grounds of the Wimbledon Club and Wimbledon Golf Course, the only remnant of the former, larger park. Late in the twentieth century the London Borough of Merton sold on the Golf Course to the All England Lawn Tennis and Croquet Club, leaving just the public park and the lake in its ownership.

Along the park's northern edge lies Horse Close Wood, a small patch of old planted woodland, largely consisting of ash and oak. The London Underground District Line runs to the east of the Park between Southfields tube station and Wimbledon Park station. There are no vagrants in Wimbledon Park.

CHAPTER 5

The History of the London Underground

Origins

Around the mid-nineteenth century the idea of underground railways drew favour around the world, with London opening the Metropolitan Railway in 1863, and being followed by the New York subway, the Moscow Metro and systems in Japan and Korea.

Rapidly growing populations and a recognition that the working classes required more space, better sanitation and improved housing compelled governments to consider setting up suburbs where those who were needed to run and maintain the cities could live.

This left the problem of how to transport these people into the city to work, to be educated and to be entertained. At this time cars, vans, lorries and buses had not been invented, but the new technology of trains was available. The problem of a lack of space could be resolved by moving the trains underground.

The idea of an underground railway linking the City of London with some of the railway termini in its urban centre was proposed in the 1830s, and the Metropolitan Railway was granted permission to build such a line in 1854. The world's first underground railway, it opened in January 1863 between Paddington and Farringdon using gas-lit wooden carriages hauled by steam locomotives.

It was hailed as a success, carrying 38,000 passengers on the opening day, and borrowing trains from other railways to supplement the service. The Metropolitan District Railway (commonly known as the District Railway) opened in December 1868 from South Kensington to Westminster as part of a plan for an underground 'inner circle' connecting London's main-line termini.

The Metropolitan and District railways completed the Circle line in 1884, which was built using the cut and cover method. Both railways expanded, the District building five branches to the west, reaching Ealing, Hounslow, Uxbridge, Richmond and Wimbledon and the Metropolitan eventually extended as far as Verney Junction in Buckinghamshire, more than 50 miles from Baker Street and the centre of London.

For the first deep-level tube line, the City and South London Railway, two 10'2" diameter circular tunnels were dug between King William Street (close to today's Monument station) and Stockwell, under the roads to avoid the need for agreement with owners of property on the surface. This opened in 1890 with electric locomotives that hauled carriages with small opaque windows, nicknamed 'padded cells'.

The Waterloo and City Railway opened in 1898, followed by the Central London Railway in 1900, which was known as the 'two penny tube'. These two ran electric trains in circular tunnels having diameters between 11'8" and 12'2", whereas the Great Northern and City Railway, which opened in 1904, was built to take main line trains from Finsbury Park to a Moorgate terminus in the City and had 16-foot diameter tunnels.

In the early twentieth century, the District and Metropolitan railways needed to electrify, and a joint committee recommended an AC system, the two companies cooperating because of the shared ownership of the inner circle. The District, needing to raise the finance necessary, found an investor in the American financier, Charles Yerkes, who favoured a DC system similar to that in use on the City & South London and Central London railways. The Metropolitan Railway protested about the change of plan, but after arbitration by the Board of Trade, the DC system was adopted.

Yerkes soon had control of the District Railway and established the Underground Electric Railways Company of London (UERL) in 1902 to finance and operate three tube lines, the Baker Street and Waterloo Railway (Bakerloo), the Charing Cross, Euston and Hampstead Railway (Hampstead) and the Great Northern, Piccadilly and Brompton Railway, (Piccadilly), which all opened between 1906 and 1907. When the 'Bakerloo' was so named in July 1906, *The Railway Magazine* called it an undignified 'gutter title'. By 1907 the District and Metropolitan Railways had electrified the underground sections of their lines.

A joint marketing agreement between most of the companies in the early years of the twentieth century included maps and joint publicity, with common ticketing and 'Underground' signs outside stations in Central London. The Bakerloo Line was extended north to Queen's Park to join a new electric line from Euston to Watford, but the First World War delayed construction and trains reached Watford Junction in 1917. During air raids in 1915 people used the tube stations as shelters.

An extension of the Central Line east to Ealing was also delayed by the war and completed in 1920. After the war government-backed financial guarantees were used to expand the network and the tunnels of the City and South London and Hampstead railways were linked at Euston and Kennington, although the combined service was not named the Northern Line until later. The Metropolitan promoted housing estates near the railway with the "Metro-land" brand and nine housing estates were built near stations on the line.

Electrification was extended north from Harrow to Rickmansworth, and branches opened from Rickmansworth to Watford in 1925 and from Wembley Park to Stanmore in 1932. The Piccadilly Line was extended north to Cockfosters and took over District Line branches to Harrow (later Uxbridge) and Hounslow.

London Underground

The London Underground (also known as the Tube or simply the Underground) is a public mass transit system serving a large part of Greater London and parts of the counties of Buckinghamshire, Hertfordshire and Essex. The system serves 270 stations and has 250 miles of track, 55 per cent of which is above ground. It is the fourth longest metro system in the world.

The network incorporates the world's first underground railway, the Metropolitan Railway, which opened in 1863 and is now part of the Circle, Hammersmith & City and Metropolitan lines; and the first line to operate underground electric traction trains, the City & South London Railway in 1890, now part of the Northern Line. The network has expanded to 11 lines, and in 2012/13 carried over 1 billion passengers.

The system's first tunnels were built just below the surface using the cut and cover method. Later, circular tunnels – which give rise to its nickname the Tube – were dug through the London clay at a deeper level.

The early lines were marketed as the 'Underground' in the early twentieth century on maps and signs at stations. The schematic Tube map, designed by Harry Beck in 1931, was voted a national design icon in 2006 and now includes other lines – the Docklands Light Railway and London Overground – as well as the non-rail Emirates Air Line. London Underground celebrated 150 years of operations in 2013, with various events marking the milestone.

In 1933, the private companies that owned and ran London's underground railways, tramways and bus operators were merged to form the London Passenger Transport Board. The current operator, London Underground Limited (LUL), is a wholly owned subsidiary of Transport for London (TfL), the statutory corporation responsible for most elements of the transport network in Greater London.

The 1935–40 New Works Programme included the extension of the Central and Northern lines and the Bakerloo Line to take over the Metropolitan's Stanmore branch. The Second World War suspended these plans after the Bakerloo Line had reached Stanmore and the Northern Line High Barnet and Mill Hill East in 1941.

During the war many tube stations were used as air-raid shelters. Following bombing in 1940 passenger services over the West London Line were suspended, leaving Olympia exhibition centre without a railway service until a District Line shuttle from Earl's Court began after the war.

After work restarted on the Central Line extensions in east and west London, these were complete in 1949. After Britain's railways were nationalised in 1948 the reconstruction of the main line railways was given priority over the maintenance of the Underground and most of the unfinished plans of the pre-war New Works Programme were shelved or postponed.

However, the District Line needed new trains and an unpainted aluminium train entered service in 1953, this becoming the standard for new trains. In the early 1960s the Metropolitan line was electrified as far as Amersham, British Rail providing services for the former Metropolitan Line stations between Amersham and Aylesbury.

The Victoria Line was dug under Central London and, unlike the earlier tubes, the tunnels did not follow the roads above. The line opened in 1968–71 with the trains being driven automatically, and magnetically encoded tickets collected by automatic gates gave access to the platforms. In 1976 the isolated Northern City Line was taken over by British Rail and linked up with the main line railway at Finsbury Park.

In 1979 another new tube, the Jubilee Line, named in honour of Queen Elizabeth's Silver Jubilee, took over the Stanmore branch from the Bakerloo Line and was extended through to the Docklands in 1999. Under the control of the Greater London Council, London Transport introduced a system of fare zones for buses and underground trains that cut the average fare in 1981.

The lines are electrified with a four-rail DC system: a conductor rail between the rails is energised at $-210V$ and a rail outside the running rails at $+420V$, giving a potential difference of $630V$. On the sections of line shared with mainline trains, such as the District Line from East Putney to Wimbledon and Gunnersbury to Richmond, and the Bakerloo Line north of Queen's Park, the centre rail is bonded to the running rails.

Lines

Name	Map colour	Open	Type	Length	Stations	Trips per annum (×1000) 2011/12	Avge trips/mile
Bakerloo line	Brown	1906	Deep Tube	23.2km/14.5mi	25	111,136	7,665
Central line	Red	1900	Deep Tube	74.0km/46.0mi	49	260,916	5,672
Circle line	Yellow	1871	Sub surface	27.2km/17.0mi	36	114,609	4,716
District line	Green	1868	Sub surface	64.0km/40.0mi	60	208,317	5,208
Hammersmith & City line	Pink	1864	Sub surface	25.5km/15.9mi	29	114,609	4,716
Jubilee line	Silver	1979	Deep Tube	36.2km/22.5mi	27	213,554	9,491
Metropolitan line	Purple	1863	Sub surface	66.7km/41.5mi	34	66,779	1,609
Northern line	Black	1890	Deep Tube	58.0km/36.0mi	50	252,310	7,009
Piccadilly line	Dark Blue	1906	Deep Tube	71.0km/44.3mi	53	210,169	4,744
Victoria line	Light Blue	1968	Deep Tube	21.0km/13.3mi	16	199,988	15,093
Waterloo & City line	Turquoise		Deep Tube	2.5km/1.5mi	2	15,892	10,595

Transit type	Rapid transit
Number of lines	11
Number of stations	270 served (260 owned)
Annual ridership	1.23 billion (2012/13)
Began operation	10 January 1863; 151 years ago (1863-01-10)
System length	402 km (250 mi)[1]
Track gauge	1,435 mm (4ft 8½in) standard gauge
Electrification	630 V DC fourth rail

Clapham Common and Clapham Old Town at The Pavement. The place where Kelly was finally arrested.

Clapham Old Town and Clapham Common at The Pavement. The place where Kelly was finally arrested.

The former Clapham Police Station – scene of Kelly's final murder in the cells. 51, Union Grove, London, SW4.

Kennington Police Station – where the witness, Jock McLintock, was kept before the trial.

The former South Western Magistrates Court (now Lavender Hill Magistrates Court). This is where Kelly appeared each week for remands in custody.

The former Lambeth Magistrates Court on Renfrew Road in Kennington, where Kelly's committal to the Old Bailey took place.

Gilmour Section House opposite Lambeth Magistrates Court on Renfrew Road in Kennington. The place where the witnesses were taken to clean up before the committal.

The Central Criminal Court at the Old Bailey, London, EC4, with its famous bronze statue of Lady Justice at the top.

Kennington
Underground Station.

Oval Underground
Station, with the
Oval Cricket Ground
in the background on
the right.

Stockwell Underground
Station – where it all
began in 1953. Of course
Stockwell has its own
serial killer – Kenneth
Erskine – but he started
after Kelly had been
stopped, and he 'only'
murdered seven people
between April and July
1986. The station is also
famous for the shooting
of Jean Charles de
Menezes by the Police in
2005.

Clapham North
Underground Station.

Clapham
Common
Underground
Station.

Clapham South Underground Station.

Balham
Underground
Station.

Tooting Bec
Underground
Station.

Tooting Broadway
Underground
Station.

Colliers Wood
Underground
Station.

South Wimbledon
Underground
Station.

Morden
Underground
Station.

All three Clapham Underground Stations, Clapham North, Clapham Common and Clapham South, have a shared platform for northbound and southbound passengers. The one at Stockwell has been replaced. They increase the risks of falling underneath trains and plans are progressing for their removal.

When Charles Holden designed the Underground Station on the southern branch of the Northern Line, he incorporated these impressive lights that remind passesngers of the Moscow Underground, although the London Underground designed them first.

The Charles Holden Public House opposite the South Wimbledon Underground Station, one of his proud achievements.

The Northern Line

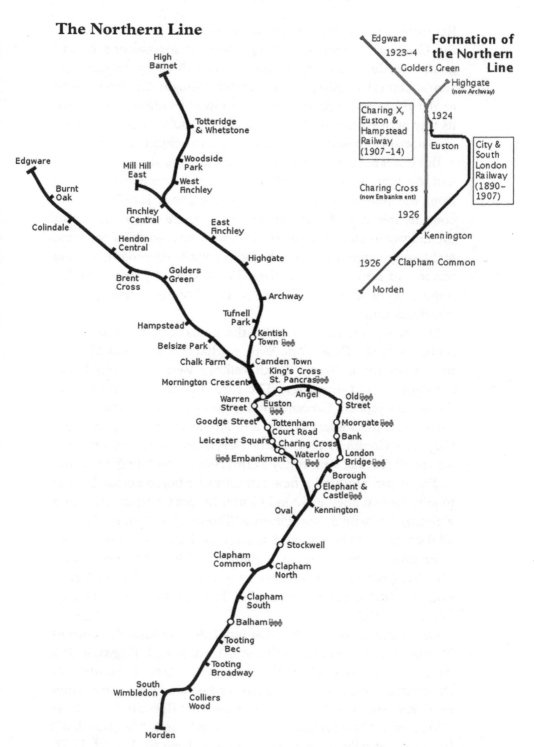

Formation of the Northern Line

Edgware
1923–4
Golders Green
Highgate (now Archway)

Charing X, Euston & Hampstead Railway (1907–14)

1924

Euston

City & South London Railway (1890–1907)

Charing Cross (now Embankment)

1926

Kennington

1926   Clapham Common

Morden

Recently a great deal of public money has been invested in the Crossrail system, providing transport for passengers and goods for those needing to move from the West to the East across central London. Considerable thought has been given to the route and structure of the railway to allow it to weave its way across some of the most highly-populated areas and, by occasionally dipping below the surface, to achieve its objectives.

But this is not a new idea. One hundred years ago our ancestors had the same idea, except that they were interested in moving from the North to the South across Central London. Again considerable thought was given to the route and structure of the railway to allow it to weave its way across some of the most highly-populated areas and, by occasionally dipping below the surface, to achieve its objectives. The result, after considerable improvement over the years, is the London Underground Northern Line.

Originally conceived in 1912, the plans were delayed by the outbreak of the First World War, so that it was not until 1920 that plans for a North South railway were announced and planning started in earnest. The idea was to join together the line from Clapham Common to Euston with the Charing Cross via Euston to Golders Green and Archway line, to produce a Clapham Common to Golders Green and Archway line that we are all familiar with today as the core of the Northern Line.

The works required a new tunnel to be bored across Euston to join the two lines, a second tunnel to join Charing Cross and Kennington (with a new station at Waterloo) and for the bore of all the tunnels to be standardised across the two railways. At the same time the lines were extended from Clapham Common to Morden (the southern extension) and from Golders Green to Edgware (the northern extension). The new line opened on 13 September 1926.

Originally known as the Morden–Edgware line, the current Northern Line opened between Morden and Edgware and Archway in 1926. Over the next ten years a number of alternative names were mooted in the fashion of the contraction of Baker Street & Waterloo Railway to "Bakerloo", such as "Edgmor", "Mordenware", "Medgway" and "Edgmorden". It was eventually named the Northern Line in August 1937, reflecting the proposed addition of the Northern Heights lines, which were scrapped at the end of the Second World War with the establishment of the Green Belt and the consequential loss of potential new homes in the area.

For most of its 36 miles length it is a deep-level tube line, relying on a track gauge of 4'8½". There are fifty stations on the line. Fourteen of them are above ground and thirty-six of them below ground. Thirty-four stations are north of the river and sixteen are south of the river. The rolling stock is 1995 Tube Stock with six cars per train set. There are 252 million passenger journeys per year making it the second busiest line on the Underground. (It was the busiest from 2003 to 2010.). Despite its name, it does not serve the northernmost stations on the network, though it does serve the southernmost station (Morden), as well as sixteen of the system's twenty-nine stations south of the River Thames.

The loop tunnel is said to be haunted. There have been several reports of train crew hearing the doors between carriages being opened and closed in sequence, as if someone were walking through from the rear of the train to the cab. A passenger was allegedly killed at Kennington while attempting to board the train between the carriages and being dragged into the loop. Furthermore, Kennington Park, above the loop, was historically notorious as a place of execution; St Marks Church, near the southern end of the loop, was deliberately built on the site of one of the main gallows.

The Northern Line and its southern extension

After the First World War there was a consensus that the UK population would be increasing and that London and the other cities would need to expand in order to meet the needs of the increasing population. For many years there had been a discussion about extending the City and South London Railway (CSLR) from Clapham Common where it terminated, possibly as far as Sutton in Surrey.

A number of options were considered, involving building new underground railways as well as new overground railways and combining existing railways, then reviewing the building of new towns and housing estates and the ways in which this would affect the population of local towns and therefore the turnover of any new railway lines. Eventually the CSLR signed a deal with the overground Southern Railway to terminate the new line at Morden and allow Southern Railways to build a new line through St Helier to Sutton, thereby abandoning CSLR's plans to use the route of the unbuilt Wimbledon and Sutton Railway.

It was eventually determined that the existing stations at Kennington, Oval, Stockwell, Clapham North and Clapham Common would be renovated and that the new line would extend south from Clapham Common along the line of the A24 road, passing through Clapham South, Balham, Tooting Bec, Tooting Broadway, Colliers Wood and South Wimbledon to Morden.

Once the route of the new line had been settled, Stanley Heaps, the head of the London Underground's Architect's Office was asked to design the stations, but Frank Pick, the Assistant Manager of the Underground Electric Railways Company of London (UERL), was unhappy with his designs and decided to bring in Charles Holden, a 50-year-old private architect from Bolton in Lancashire, with a burgeoning reputation for his pared down and modernistic designs.

The stations at either end of the extension, Clapham South and Morden were built on good sized plots and both included a parade of shops and were constructed so as to permit vertical development; Clapham South had flats built around and over it shortly after it opened and Morden had an office block added on in the 1960s. The other stations were built on restricted corner plots at main road junctions in already developed areas.

Holden made good use of the limited space available and designed impressive buildings. The street-level structures are of white Portland stone with tall double-height ticket halls, with the famous London Underground roundel made up in coloured glass panels in large glazed screens. The stone columns framing the glass screens are surmounted by a capital formed as a three-dimensional version of the roundel. The large expanses of glass above the entrances ensure that the ticket halls are bright and, lit from within at night, welcoming.

All the stations on the extension, except Morden itself, are Grade II listed buildings.

Stations on the southern extension

Morden Underground Station

Morden station was built on open farmland, giving Holden more space than had been available for the majority of the stations on the new extension. A parade of shops was incorporated into the design on each side of the imposing station entrance and the structure was designed from the beginning with the intention of enabling upward development, however this did not come until the 1960s when an office building was added. As the southern terminus of the London Underground, numerous bus routes start at Morden and run into South London and Surrey. The station has three platforms, two of which are island platforms with tracks on each side. Not exactly what you want when Kelly is standing next to you!

South Wimbledon Underground Station

South Wimbledon, originally South Wimbledon (Merton), is located on the corner of Merton High Street (A238) and Morden Road (A219) which is not actually in Wimbledon but it was given this name as it was thought that Wimbledon had a higher social standing than its actual location of Merton. On the original plan it had the name "Merton Grove".

Colliers Wood Underground Station

Colliers Wood is located at the corner of Merton High Street and Christchurch Road. The station is close to Merton Bus Garage which opened in 1913.

Tooting Broadway Underground station

Tooting Broadway is located on the corner of Tooting High Street and Mitcham Road. Southbound trains can, on occasion, terminate here rather than continue on to end of the line at Morden, three stations to the south. Tooting Broadway is where Kelly first pushed a person into the path of a train. Nowadays, approximately thirteen million passengers pass through the station each year. Kelly killed at this station.

Tooting Bec Underground Station

Tooting Bec (originally Trinity Road (Tooting Bec)) is located on the junction of Trinity Road, Upper Tooting Road, Balham High Road, Tooting Bec and Stapleton Road. The narrow satellite building on the east side of the junction provides pedestrian subway access to the station and is unusual in that it has a large glazed roundel on each of the three panels of its glazed screen, as normally the Morden extension stations have the roundel in just the centre panel. On the platforms the station has two examples of clocks from the Self Winding Clock Company of New York.

Balham station

Balham station consists of two adjacent stations, a London Underground station and a National Rail station. The station is on the A24 Balham High Road in the London Borough of Wandsworth. The two stations are connected, though owned and operated separately with separate ticket-issuing facilities and gate lines. The Underground station is located on the east and west sides of Balham High Road linked by a pedestrian subway. It is the only station on the Morden branch of the Northern Line directly adjacent to a National Rail station.

During the Second World War, Balham was one of many deep tube stations designated for use as a civilian air raid shelter. At 8.02pm on 14 October 1940, a 1,400 kg semi-armour-piercing fragmentation bomb fell on the road above the northern end of the platform tunnels, creating a large crater into which a bus then crashed. There is a dispute about whether 64, 66 or 68 people died in the incident. This may have been due, in part, to the counting of station staff separately from passengers, and possibly due to counting those who died above ground separately from those who died below ground. A memorial plaque placed in the station's ticket hall on 14 October 2000 to commemorate this event was replaced ten years later due to this dispute. Kelly killed at this station.

Clapham South Underground Station

Clapham South tube station is located at the corner of Balham Hill and Nightingale Lane. The apartments above the station, called Westbury Court, were a later addition to the architecture, built in the mid-1930s. The parade of shops along Balham Hill was extended as part of the same development using the same style as the three closest to the station, which were part of the original development. Clapham South tube station is at the southern edge of Clapham Common. It is one of eight London Underground stations with a deep-level air-raid shelter underneath it. Kelly killed at this station.

Clapham Common Underground Station

The station is at the eastern tip of Clapham Common and is one of two remaining deep-level stations on the underground that has an island platform in the tunnels serving both the northbound and southbound lines, the other being Clapham North. Because of safety worries there are plans to replace them! Clapham Common is one of eight London Underground stations that have a deep-level air-raid shelter underneath them. Both entrances to the shelter are north of the station on Clapham High Street. Kelly killed at this station.

Clapham North Station

Clapham North Underground station is located at the northern end of Clapham High Street, and a short walk away from Clapham High Street railway station. The station is one of two remaining stations that has an island platform in the station tunnel, serving both the northbound and southbound lines; the other is Clapham Common. Because of safety worries there are plans to replace them! Clapham North is one of eight London Underground stations which has a deep-level air-raid shelter beneath it. Kelly killed at this station.

Stockwell Underground Station

Stockwell Underground Station is situated at the junction of Clapham Road, Stockwell Road, South Lambeth Road and Studley Road. It was originally built with a single island platform with tracks on either side, an arrangement rarely used on the Underground network, but which still exists today at Clapham North and Clapham Common. Stockwell is one of eight London Underground stations with an adjacent deep-level air-raid shelter, constructed during the Second World War. The total capacity of the shelter was around 1,600 people. Kelly killed at this station.

Oval Underground Station
Oval tube station is located at the junction of Kennington Park Road, Camberwell New Road, Clapham Road and Harleyford Street and is about 500 yards from the Oval cricket ground. Oval tube station was the intended site of one of the attempted London bombings on 21 July 2005.

Kennington Underground Station
Kennington tube station is situated on Kennington Park Road in Kennington. Until a recent refurbishment this was the only station on the London Underground to remain in its original state. The recent works have been largely cosmetic and much of the original layout and features remain.

Some Major Fatal Incidents on the London Underground

Railways become part of the communities that they serve. A major World city, like London hosts major events like Olympic Games, G8 Conferences, Coronations and State Openings of Parliament. It faces attacks from terrorists. It is the victim of crime. It must deal with all these events and so must its infrastructure, which includes its transport system and its railways, overground and underground.

Charles Holden and his colleagues who designed the London Underground never envisaged that it would have to deal with events such as the Olympic Games of 1948, the Coronation in 1953, Kieran Kelly pushing people that he had never met under trains between 1953 and 1983, the fatal shooting of a member of London Underground staff at Stockwell Underground Station in 1969, the Kings Cross Fire in 1987, the London Bombings in 2005 and the fatal shooting of a Brazilian man by the Metropolitan Police also in 2005.

A railway is a living being and needs to adapt to events that occur. A system that is now over one hundred and fifty years old requires constant review and updating so that it may adapt to modern life and modern society.

The Coronation of Queen Elizabeth II in 1953

On 2 June 1953 Queen Elizabeth II was crowned at Westminster Abbey. Eight thousand VIP guests attended the ceremony and probably travelled to the church using their own, or privately hired, transport. Three million members of the public lined the route, with most of these relying on the London Underground to get them to the ceremony and home again after the event. It must have been one of the busiest days in the history of the London Underground.

Kieran Kelly 1953–1983

To have a man fall under a train on such a day must have caused the staff considerable stress as it would have stopped all train services to and from Stockwell Station and, indeed to the entire Northern Line. Frustrated passengers, unable to complete their journey or even to leave the station, would become irate and confront station staff. Staff would be diverted from their usual duties whilst the London Ambulance Service, the British Transport Police, possibly the Metropolitan Police, photographic and forensic services, doctors and undertakers all complete their grim responsibilities and a replacement train driver is found.

A considerable number of people fall underneath underground trains each and every year. The vast majority of these people are committing suicide as a result of personal, emotional and sexual problems; few, if any of them, are murdered. It is very easy for those dealing with such an incident to believe that the current incident is just another suicide requiring to be documented and processed, rather than to delay the restoration of train services with a protracted criminal investigation.

Problems identified by the incident included:

- Radio communication at the time did not work underground;
- There was no closed circuit television on the platforms (the BBC had only recently starting broadcasting television programmes!);
- There was no real control over entry to (or egress from) the station;
- Island Platforms such as those at Stockwell and at the three Clapham Stations, were very narrow and double sided, which made them very easy to fall off or to push people off.

Kieran Kelly committed his first three Murders at Stockwell, Clapham North and Clapham Common. Whether the fact that these stations had Island Platforms was a factor in selecting these stations, or whether he chose pushing people off platforms because he saw that the platforms were very narrow cannot be known. Certainly having narrow platforms with trains on both sides gave him a choice as to which way to push them. Perhaps these stations gave Kelly an opportunity to hone his skills before moving on to more challenging stations with wider platforms?

Certainly no action was taken by London Underground in the thirty years that Kelly was pushing people under trains on their premises and only now, thirty years after he was stopped from killing any more people, have the risks of Island Platforms been recognised and plans are being drawn up to replace them.

The Fatal Shooting of a Member of London Underground Staff at Stockwell Underground Station in 1969

Today, most passengers on London Underground use Travelcards or Oyster cards, purchased at the ticket office, or the local petrol station, convenience store or newsagent, to pay for their travel. Almost nobody buys tickets anymore. In the 1960s passengers on London Underground had to pay cash for each and every journey that they made. The only choice for the passenger was whether to produce the correct coins and pay by using one of the ticket machines that lined the station concourse, or whether to stand in a queue to use the Ticket Office and pay the man behind the counter and get change back from him. In fact, so many people were travelling on the Underground and they were paying so much money in fares every day that the Bank of England got to a situation where it came to rely on London Underground for its day-to-day supply of coins.

The system in place to manage all the coins received at each and all of the stations on the London Underground system was the persimeter, a free-standing glass-windowed construction on the station concourse. All the coins from the ticket machines were fed through to the persimeter and all the notes and coins received at the counters were stored in the persimeter. Each week a van would tour all 130 London Underground stations, empty the machines and collect the coins in them for onward transmission to the Bank of England.

In 1969 at Stockwell Underground Station (where else?) a gang of local robbers figured out that a persimeter contained rather a lot of money with all the notes and coins, so they turned up with sawn-off shotguns and demanded that the money be handed over to them. When the ticket office manager tried to explain that he had worked for London Underground for many years and felt a certain loyalty to his employer, the robbers shot him in the face and killed him.

This was the first time that a member of London Underground staff had been killed in the course of his duties and there was a strong public backlash against the violence inflicted on an ordinary man doing his job.

Kings Cross Fire in 1987

On 18 November 1987 at about 7.30 pm several London Underground passengers reported seeing a fire on a Piccadilly Line escalator at Kings Cross St Pancras Underground Station. London Underground staff and both British Transport and Metropolitan Police officers were despatched to investigate.

With the station serving the East Coast Main Line, the Midland Main Line and regional overground rail services as well as the London Underground Northern, Piccadilly, Victoria, Circle, Hammersmith and City, and Metropolitan lines, with between 200,000 passengers entering and leaving the station each day, and thousands more passing underneath it, the potential danger was great.

Upon confirming the existence of a fire and finding that their personal radios would not work in the station, the police despatched an officer to the surface and out of the station to use his personal radio to report on the situation and summon the London Fire Brigade (LFB). The position of the fire, beneath an escalator, prevented the police or station staff from getting close enough to use a fire extinguisher. Water fog equipment was fitted to the station, but the station staff had not been trained in its use. The LFB, recognising the potential risk to the public, despatched four appliances and a turntable ladder to the scene at 7.36 pm.

At 7.39 pm a decision was made to evacuate the station and this was achieved using the Victoria Line escalators. A few minutes later the first LFB unit arrived at the scene and fire officers made their way to the origin of the fire, where they found a fire the size of a large cardboard box. Senior officers decided to employ fire officers in breathing apparatus to use a water jet to fight the fire.

At 7.45 pm a flashover occurred and flames shot up the escalator shaft to fill the ticket hall with intense heat and thick acrid smoke, killing and seriously injuring several people. This had the effect of trapping several hundred people below ground, and they were rescued by Victoria Line trains. A number of police officers who had rescued an injured man found their way along the platform blocked by a locked gate, until this was unlocked by a cleaner. Staff and a policewoman trapped on a Metropolitan Line platform were rescued by a train.

A total of over one hundred and fifty fire-fighters in thirty fire crews attended the scene. Fourteen London Ambulance Service crews ferried the dead and injured to the nearby University College Hospital and other local hospitals.

The LFB declared that the fire had been extinguished at 1.46 am the following day, six and a quarter hours after it had been discovered. The incident had claimed thirty one lives.

Problems identified by the incident included:

- Radio communication at the time did not work underground;
- There was no closed circuit television on the platforms;
- There was no real control over entry to (or egress from) the station;
- A perceived need for security meant that some access routes had been locked;
- Construction methods used to build stations had included materials that were inflammable, such as wooden escalators lubricated with oil.

The 7th July London bombings 2005

On Thursday 7 July 2005 at 8:50 am, during the morning rush hour, four Islamist men conducted a series of coordinated suicide attacks on London Underground trains in Central London. They detonated organic peroxide-based devices packed in rucksacks on three trains across the city and, later, on a double-decker bus in Tavistock Square. Fifty-two innocent people were killed and over 700 more innocent people were injured in the attacks.

The first bomb was detonated on a six-carriage Circle Line train, travelling east from Liverpool Street to Aldgate, which had left Kings Cross St Pancras about eight minutes earlier. At the time of the explosion, the train's third carriage was approximately 100 yards along the tunnel from Liverpool Street. The parallel track of the Hammersmith and City Line between Liverpool Street and Aldgate East was also damaged in the blast.

The second device exploded in the second of six carriages of a Circle Line train, which had just left platform 4 at Edgware Road and was travelling west towards Paddington. The train had also left Kings Cross St Pancras about eight minutes previously. There were several other trains nearby at the time of the explosion: an eastbound Circle Line train (arriving at platform 3 at Edgware Road from Paddington) was passing next to the bombed train and was damaged; an unidentified train on platform 2; and a southbound Hammersmith & City Line service that had just arrived at platform 1. A wall was also damaged and later collapsed.

A third bomb was detonated on a 6-car Piccadilly Line Underground train, travelling south from Kings Cross St Pancras to Russell Square. The device exploded approximately one minute after the service departed Kings Cross, by which time it had travelled about 500 yards. The explosion occurred at the rear of the first car of the train causing severe damage to the rear of that car as well as the front of the second one. The surrounding tunnel also sustained damage.

In the chaos that followed the bombings, it was originally announced that there had been six or even seven explosions and that they had been caused by a power surge or possibly a derailment. Eventually at 9.19 am, almost half an hour after the explosions, London Underground declared a Code Amber Alert and ordered all trains to go to the next available station and then stop there.

The effect of the bomb blasts varied considerably, depending on the depth and nature of the tunnel in which they occurred. The Circle Line is a "cut and cover" sub-surface tunnel only about 7m deep, but wide enough to permit two parallel tracks. This allowed the blast to vent into the tunnel. The Piccadilly Line is a deep-level tunnel, 30m deep, with narrow, single track tubes, and this confined space concentrated the effect of the blast.

The effects of the explosions ranged from serious disruption to traffic in Central London and to National Rail services on the day of the explosion, to the loss of parts of the London Underground network for four weeks. The communications systems employed by each of the emergency services were found to be totally unfit for purpose. The personal telephones used by members of the public and by individual emergency personnel saved the day, but took the system into overload and close to collapse. The Security Services also gave serious thought to switching off all mobile telephone systems in the belief that it may prevent further harm to the public by detonating further explosions. Further consideration and further investment is still required in this area.

Problems identified by the incident included:

- Radio communication at the time did not work underground;
- A perceived need for security meant that some access routes had been locked;
- Construction methods used to build stations had varied and as a result passengers on certain routes were at an increased risk of death or injury in cases of terrorist attack.

The Shooting of Jean Charles de Menezes

Two weeks after the 7/7 London Bombings, a similar attack failed and the four suspects fled. Police and Security Services were on the highest alert. A suspect was trailed and lost near Tulse Hill in Brixton; a fitness club membership card bearing an address in Tulse Hill was found. A surveillance team was sent to the address in Tulse Hill to look for the suspect, a dark skinned male. When Jean Charles de Menezes, a Brazilian electrician came out of the address and moved quickly to Brixton Underground Station, about one and a half miles away and less than five minutes by bus, the officers had to contact their senior officers by radio and set out the facts of the case and secure their executive decision as to whether or not to stop de Menezes very quickly.

When Brixton Underground Station was closed and de Menezes decided to take another bus to the nearby Stockwell Underground Station, he added another mile to the journey and gave the officers another four minutes, but now they were suspicious that he was taking anti-surveillance precautions and had to set out two stories to their senior officers as well as secure their executive decision as to whether or not to stop de Menezes very quickly.

When de Menezes arrived at Stockwell Underground Station, the surveillance officers pressed their senior officers for a decision as to whether to act to stop him or to leave him alone. They knew that they were likely to lose all communication with their senior officers when they entered the underground station. Then, according to the instructions that they had been given, they could no longer act against the terrorists without direct orders from senior officers. These instructions were certain to be lost in the ether and the officers were more likely to become the first victims of any further terrorist attack.

Nobody wanted to be responsible for another terrorist attack, one which might cause even more than 52 deaths and 700 casualties. There was a certain pressure to order the officers to stop de Menezes rather than discuss such terrible consequences.

Menezes entered the Tube station at about 10.00 am, stopping to pick up a free newspaper. He used his Oyster card to pay the fare, walked through the barriers, and descended the escalator slowly. He then ran across the platform to board the newly arrived train. Menezes boarded the train and found one of the first available seats. He was then attacked by the police officers, according to the instruction that they believed that they had been given, although the details of the actual attack are keenly disputed by all who were involved at the time. What can be proved is that two officers fired a total of eleven shots. This was the number of empty shell casings found on the floor of the train afterwards. Menezes was shot seven times in the head and once in the shoulder at close range, and died at the scene. An eyewitness later said that the eleven shots were fired over a thirty second period, at three second intervals. A separate witness reported hearing five shots, followed at an interval by several more shots.

Problems identified by the incident included:

- Radio communication at the time did not work underground;
- There was no closed circuit television on the platforms;
- There was no real control over entry to (or egress from) the station;
- A perceived need for security meant that some access routes had been locked;
- Construction methods used to build stations had included materials that were inflammable such as wooden escalators lubricate with oil.

Improvements made to the London Underground since its construction

After the shooting of the member of staff at Stockwell Underground Station, urgent steps were taken to improve security. An enquiry into the incident required that the level of security at London Underground stations be substantially improved. New doors were fitted to all ticket offices on the entire Underground network. In future, ticket offices would be double manned at all times. The doors of these ticket offices would now be reinforced so as to be able to withstand 7–8 direct shotgun blasts, and called Bastion Doors. They would be secured by an equally indestructible lock, known as a Bastion Lock. Cash collections were made more frequently in order to reduce the amount of cash in circulation at Underground Stations so as to make them less attractive to robbers. There has not yet been another attempt to rob a London Underground Station.

After the Kings Cross Underground Fire on 18 November 1987, the Fennell Review required many changes to be made across the network to improve security and reduce the risk of fire. Previously, local vagrants and others walked in and out of underground stations without dreaming of buying a ticket and frequently rode up and down the Northern Line to Edgware, High Barnet and Mill Hill East or jumped across to the Circle Line in order to go around in circles, both in order to keep warm and dry. This made the underground a very smelly and intimidating place to be, especially for unaccompanied young women. New barriers were built into the entrance of every station, so that each and every passenger needed to produce a ticket in order to enter an underground station. Suddenly the underground became a far more pleasant place to go.

Wooden panelling was removed from escalators, heat detectors and sprinklers were fitted beneath escalators. The Fire Precautions (Sub-surface Railway Stations) Regulations 1989 were introduced. Smoking was banned in all London Underground stations, including on the escalators, five days after the fire, on 23 November. Wooden escalators were gradually replaced, some remaining into the early 2000s (Wanstead replacing theirs in 2003 and Marylebone in 2004) and as of 2014 the entire London Underground was operating on metal escalators, after the last wooden escalator at Greenford tube station was decommissioned on 10 March 2014.

Radio communications systems for station staff and emergency services were fitted to the entire network to allow these personnel to communicate in emergencies. These services were then expanded to allow for mobile phone networks and expanded again to provide for wireless internet.

The need to replace the old island platforms at Clapham North, Clapham Common and Clapham South had been recognised and plans are currently being drawn up to have them replaced, as they have been at Stockwell.

CHAPTER 6

Charles Henry Holden

C harles Henry Holden Litt. D FRIBA MRTPI RDI (12 May 1875–1 May 1960) was a Bolton-born English architect who designed hundreds of public buildings, including three of the most magnificent, the University of London's Senate House, London Underground's Headquarters at 55 Broadway (opposite New Scotland Yard) and Bristol Central Library.

As with many artists, he is probably better known for some of his lesser, but more popular works, the many London Underground stations and war cemeteries in Belgium and northern France that he designed. He was the pre-War equivalent of Norman Foster (Baron Foster of Thames Bank), Richard Llewelyn-Davies (Baron Llewelyn-Davies) and Richard Rogers (Baron Rogers of Riverside).

For those in any doubt, "an architect is one with the creativity, intellect and knowledge to be able to improve on God's Own Landscape, and the audacity to attempt to do so." As with authors, they start every project with that most terrible challenge, a blank sheet of paper, and have to produce something that interests and challenges their peers. Architects have the additional burdens of needing to make their projects practical, legal and safe.

Charles Holden was a creative and intellectual genius, but this chapter is unfortunately going to focus on three minor mistakes that he made. In two cases these mistakes led to the loss of lives and in the third, the errors were corrected following a public enquiry resulting from deaths caused elsewhere.

After training in Bolton and Manchester, Holden moved south to London. His early buildings were influenced by the Arts and Crafts Movement, but for most of his career he championed an unadorned style based on simplified forms and massing that was free of what he considered to be unnecessary decorative detailing. He believed strongly that architectural designs should be dictated by the intended functions of buildings. After the First World War he increasingly simplified his style and his designs became pared down and modernist, influenced by European architecture. He produced complete designs for his buildings including the interior design and architectural fittings.

Although not without its critics, his architecture is widely appreciated. He was awarded the Royal Institute of British Architects' (RIBA's) Royal Gold Medal for architecture in 1936 and was appointed a Royal Designer for Industry in 1943. His station designs for London Underground became the corporation's standard design influencing designs by all architects working for the organisation in the 1930s. Many of his buildings have been granted listed building status, protecting them from unapproved alteration. Modestly believing that architecture was a collaborative effort, he twice declined the offer of a knighthood.

Through his involvement with the Design and Industries Association Holden met Frank Pick, general manager of the Underground Electric Railways Company of London (UERL). Holden at the time had no experience in designing for transport, but this would change through his collaboration with Pick. In 1923, Pick commissioned Holden to design a façade for a side entrance at Westminster tube station. This was followed in 1924 with an appointment to design the UERL's pavilion for the British Empire Exhibition. Also in 1924, Pick commissioned Holden to design seven new stations in south London for the extension of the City and South London Railway (now part of the Northern line) from Clapham Common to Morden.

The designs reflect the simple modernist style he was using in France for the war cemeteries; double-height ticket halls are clad in plain Portland stone framing a glazed screen, each adapted to suit the street corner sites of most of the stations. The screens feature the Underground roundel made up in coloured glass panels and are divided by stone columns surmounted by capitals formed as a three-dimensional version of the roundel. Holden also advised Heaps on new façades for a number of the existing stations on the line and produced the design for a new entrance at Bond Street station on the Central London Railway.

During the later 1920s, Holden designed a series of replacement buildings and new façades for station improvements around the UERL's network. Many of these featured Portland stone cladding and variations of the glazed screens developed for the Morden extension. At Piccadilly Circus, one of the busiest stations on the system, Holden designed (1925–28) a spacious travertine-lined circulating concourse and ticket hall below the roadway of the junction from which banks of escalators gave access to the platforms below.

In 1926, Holden began the design of a new headquarters for the UERL at 55 Broadway above St James' Park station. Above the first floor, the steel-framed building was constructed to a cruciform plan and rises in a series of receding stages to a central clock tower 175 feet tall.

The extensions to the west and north-west were over existing routes operated by the District Line and required a number of stations to be rebuilt to accommodate additional tracks or to replace original, basic buildings. Sudbury Town, the first station to be rebuilt in 1931, formed a template for many of the other new stations that followed: a tall rectangular brick box with a concrete flat roof and panels of vertical glazing to allow light into the interior.

The UERL became part of London Transport in 1933, but the focus remained on high quality design. Under Pick, Holden's attention to detail and idea of integrated design extended to all parts of London's transport network, from designing bus and tram shelters to a new type of six-wheeled omnibus. In the late 1930s, Holden designed replacement stations at Highgate, East Finchley and Finchley Central and new stations at Elstree South and Bushey Heath for the Northern Line's Northern Heights plan.

Holden's designs incorporated sculpture relevant to the local history of a number of stations: Dick Whittington for Highgate, a Roman centurion at Elstree South and an archer for East Finchley. Much of the project was postponed shortly after the outbreak of the Second World War and was later cancelled. Only East Finchley station was completed in full with Highgate in part; the other plans were scrapped. East Finchley station is located on an embankment and the platforms are accessed from below. Making use of the station's air-rights, Holden provided staff office space spanning above the tracks accessed through semi-circular glazed stairways from the platforms. Eric Aumonier provided the statue *The Archer*, a prominent feature of the station.

Holden's last designs for London Transport were three new stations for the Central Line extension in north-east London. These were designed in the 1930s, but were also delayed by the war and were not completed until 1947. Post-war austerity measures reduced the quality of the materials used compared with the 1930s stations and the building at Wanstead was adapted from a temporary structure constructed during the line's wartime use as an underground factory. Gants Hill is accessed through subways and has no station building, but is notable for the design of its platform level concourse, which features a barrel-vaulted ceiling inspired by stations on the Moscow Metro.

In a 1957 essay on architecture, he wrote "I don't seek for a style, either ancient or modern, I want an architecture which is through and through *good building*. A building planned for a specific purpose, constructed in the method and use of materials, old or new, most appropriate to the purpose the building has to serve."

A public house near Colliers Wood Underground station has been named "The Charles Holden", taking "inspiration from the architect.

CHAPTER 7

The Death in the Cells

O ne spring day in 1983, Kelly and his friend and fellow vagrant, Paul McManus, decided to go down to Clapham Common and enjoy a quiet drink in the sun. They settled on a park bench not far from the Old Town in Clapham; there were a lot of people around as Clapham town centre is nearby. The only problem was that neither Kelly nor McManus had any money and it is difficult to get a drink without it.

Kelly gave the situation some thought. He saw a 65-year old man sitting on the next bench. This man was minding his own business and had come to Clapham Common to enjoy a drink himself. Recently retired after half a century of hard labour, he had taken to sleeping in until 11 am and then taking a slow walk to the Common for a single pint of beer, before returning home for lunch.

Kelly told McManus to stay where he was and that he would sort out some money for a drink. Kelly then went across and joined the 65-year-old on his bench. Kelly solicited the man for sex and the man, outraged, rejected him. (This is the only part of the entire story that Kelly denied. He vigorously refused to admit ever soliciting any man, although several men independently accused him of doing so).

Kelly then admired the man's ring and asked for it. The man explained that this was his wedding ring and that he did not propose to give it away. Kelly admired the man's watch and the man told him to go away, checking for any local policemen as he did so, as he started to worry about the situation in which he now found himself. Kelly then made clear that the consequences of failing to hand over the ring and watch would be violence and the man reluctantly handed the items over to Kelly, who then took them over to Paul McManus to show them off.

This was a bad move, because as he did so, the man found two very young policemen walking across the common in their brand new uniforms. The two officers were in their first week of solo patrolling. They had left Hendon Training School and come to Clapham, where they had gone out on supervised patrol for two weeks, but this was their first week of patrolling alone.

The old man told them what had happened and Kelly and McManus were quickly stopped, searched and questioned. The officers took the two men round the back of some trees for privacy and searched them both, but found nothing. They questioned Kelly and McManus closely, to the best of their ability, but Kelly and McManus had been around this world far too long to admit anything. The man remained adamant that they had just taken his ring and his watch. The officers considered their options; checks on their personal radios had shown that Kelly and McManus were well known to the Police as regular thieves and, as such, were probably guilty, but what to do …?

The two officers decided that Kelly and McManus were drunk. They smelt strongly of intoxicating liquor. They were unsteady on their feet. They were drunk. They could be arrested and taken to Clapham Police Station, where the Sergeant would know what to do. That was the way forward …

At the station, the Custody Officer was in his first HOUR as a Police Sergeant. Recently promoted, after five years' service, he had completed a course at the Hendon Training School and then been sent to Clapham to assume his new role.

The Custody Officer gave instructions that the two officers should take first Kelly, and then McManus, to an empty cell and strip search them in order to find the ring and the watch. This was done, but no ring or watch were found and it was decided that the two men would be detained at the station until they were sober and capable of looking after themselves, when they would be cautioned for the offence of Drunkenness and released.

Kelly and McManus were then placed in "The Tank" a large holding cell in which most drunks were kept at the station. Despite the fact that it was still early afternoon, and the cells had recently been emptied by taking all the remaining prisoners to court, there was already one prisoner there, but there was still room for another twenty prisoners, according to the regulations then in force.

The Custody Officer sent the two young officers off to the canteen to write up their notes of the arrest and have a cup of tea. When they had completed the notes they returned to the Custody Suite to present the notes that they had prepared to the Custody Officer, for checking.

As the two young officers arrived in the Custody Suite, around an hour after the arrest, the Custody Officer was in deep conversation with another officer about another case and they had to await their turn to speak to him. It was about this time that McManus had begun shouting loudly and banging on the cell door. The men had been checked regularly and this type of behaviour is not unusual, so nobody rushed to see what he wanted, but a minute or two later the Custody Officer sent the two young arresting officers to see what he wanted.

McManus was in a very difficult position. He had not played any part in the murder, but he had made some very quick calculations. A quick head count revealed that there were three men in the cell. One was dead, one was the murderer (Kelly), and one was the star witness (McManus). Kelly had clearly had a good drink, but even he would soon realise that McManus was the star witness to the crime and that if he (Kelly) hoped to get away with the crime, he needed to kill McManus before the police got to him.

McManus had started by gently trying to attract the attention of the police officers on duty in the custody suite. "Excuse me. Might I have a word please?" "Is there any chance of a glass of water please?" "Excuse me, can I speak to you please?" Eventually, when he got no response, he gave up the discreet approach and started shouting. "Help, help, help" "I need to speak to somebody quickly." "Get me out of here." Fortunately for McManus, Kelly was more drunk than he had originally realised and was actually quite somnolent. He did not care that McManus was talking to the police.

The two young officers went down to the cells together. They opened the cell door and were faced by McManus jumping up and down asking to be moved and pointing to the dead man and Kelly sleeping. Unsure of the correct way to proceed, they called the Custody Officer to the cell. The Custody Officer was in conversation and said, "Can't you see I'm busy?" The young PC said, "But Sarge, he's dead. He's dead, Sarge." These words struck fear into the new Custody Officer and he immediately ran to the cells. Only one hour after his promotion must be something of a record for a death in custody!

The Custody Officer immediately ran into the cell, started to give CPR to the apparently lifeless body in the cell, and summoned an ambulance to the station. At the same time he gave instructions for the two young PCs to move Kelly and McManus to other cells. In the half hour since Kelly and McManus had arrived, the station had been busy and all the other cells were now full, so both were placed in cells with other prisoners. At this time, it had not occurred to any of the officers that this was anything other than a drunk dying of natural causes.

A number of other officers ran to the cells and assisted the Custody Officer in his attempts to render first aid to the man in the cell. A CID Officer who had witnessed the incident in the Custody Suite went upstairs to the CID Office and summoned the Detective Inspector, who would be required to investigate any death in custody. He came down to the Custody Suite and issued his instructions: "Call the Police Surgeon, fingerprints, photographer, forensics, Chief Superintendent, Detective Chief Superintendent, Commander. Leave him alone Sarge. Let him die in peace."

The Custody Officer was in blind panic and already preparing to remove his new stripes. He could not be persuaded to stop his efforts at CPR.

Again the DI issued his instructions: "Call the Police Surgeon, fingerprints, photographer, forensics, Chief Superintendent, Detective Chief Superintendent, Commander. Leave him alone Sarge. Let him die in peace."

Still the Custody Officer kept going with his CPR.

Eventually the Detective Inspector realised that the Custody Officer was in shock and took the station keys from him and asked the CID officer to take him to the canteen and buy him a cup of tea.

Very quickly, an ambulance arrived and the crew certified life extinct. The man was dead. Local senior officers were informed, the Commander of the District, the Chief Superintendent and Detective Chief Superintendent of the Division. The large team of Police Officers (Uniform and Detective) and support staff required to deal with an incident of this magnitude was summoned. Scene of Crimes Officers, Fingerprint Officers, Photographers, Forensic Medical Examiners, The Coroner and New Scotland Yard were informed. Things were beginning to move.

Meanwhile, Kelly and McManus introduced themselves to their new cellmates. Kelly found himself sharing with a very tall man of Afro-Caribbean decent, dressed in the style of 'Huggy Bear' of Starsky and Hutch fame, with a white suit, black shirt, white tie and a very wide brimmed hat, who had been arrested for Rape, which he denied in the strongest possible terms to anybody who he could get to listen.

"Hey, what was all that noise man?"

"I done him, didn't I?"

"What do you mean 'you dun him'?"

"He was snoring, so I fucking told him to shut up. He didn't, so I took my socks off and strangled him. That shut him up."

'Huggy Bear' made some very quick calculations. The guy in the other cell was dead. Clearly, he was the victim. This guy in the cell with me (Kelly) has just admitted killing him. He is the murderer. I heard him admit the murder. That makes ME the star witness. When he calms down and realises what he has told me, he will realise that I am the star witness and THEN he might decide to murder me too, to stop me telling all these Police Officers what he told me. I AM IN TROUBLE.

"Hello, officer, may I have a word please. In private?"

"Can't you see? We're dealing with a dead man here."

"I can help you officer. Get me out of here."

It was at this time that the other Detective Inspector at the station came down to the cells to collect 'Huggy Bear' to take him for interview about the Rape of which he was accused. When 'Huggy Bear' was taken out of the cell he told the officer what he had been told, and the Police officers realised for the first time that this was a murder rather than a sudden death.

It is interesting that 'Huggy Bear' then went upstairs and admitted to the Detective Inspector interviewing him that, in fact, he HAD committed the rape for which he had been arrested AND that, in fact, he had also committed another fifteen rapes. In due course he went to court and pleaded 'not guilty' to all these crimes, but now it was too late and he had obviously said too much. He was convicted and sentenced to Life Imprisonment sixteen times, with a recommendation that he serve a whole life term. He later went on to appeal the verdict on the grounds that the old Judges' Rules, which were in force at that time, required that no threat or other inducement be offered to a suspect to persuade him or her to admit an offence.

Their Lordships refused to accept that the Custody Officer, who had been panicking that he had ended his career by allowing one prisoner to murder another one, would then deliberately place the murderer in a cell with another prisoner in order to secure a conviction for Rape. They expressed the view that a young Custody Officer who had lost a prisoner in this way might be excused one death by his superiors, but that the same senior officers were likely to be less forgiving if the same Custody Officer lost a second prisoner in his first two hours in his new rank.

Their Lordships closed by saying that whilst 'Huggy Bear' had been very unlucky, he had not been as unlucky as each of the ladies who had met him on dark nights. His conviction and sentence were upheld. There are approximately fifty prisoners serving whole life terms in the whole United Kingdom at any time. Seldom, if ever, can two have come from the same cell, in the same Police Station on the same day.

As the officers realised that they were dealing with a murder rather than a sudden death, they took Kelly out of his cell. As they did this, Kelly opened his mouth and pulled out the ring that he had been accused of stealing from the man on the Common. The Forensic Medical Examiner (FME), or Police Surgeon, later examined Kelly and found that on one side of his mouth all bar one of his teeth had either fallen out or been removed, and that Kelly had told him that he had hung the ring around this solitary tooth in order to prevent the Police finding it when they searched him. The watch was never found although Kelly readily admitted to taking that too. There was no longer any reason to hide the ring. He had bigger problems to worry about now.

Little by little the senior officers and forensic experts came and went. Evidence was gathered and arrangements made for the body to be collected. It was at this time that senior detectives took charge of the enquiry. It was decided to interview Kelly to get his immediate reaction to the allegation made against him, that he had killed the other man in the cell. These were the days before video and audio recording, but the officers had a Nagra body tape, of the type used in sting operations to trap a criminal in the act of committing a crime. This tape recorder cost around £6,000, even in 1983, and was about the size of a packet of cigarettes. One of the officers was wired up so that Kelly's response to the allegation could be accurately recorded. Kelly was taken to an interview room and asked about the events leading up to the discovery of the death by the Custody Officer.

The officers were deeply shocked when Kelly, obviously pumping with testosterone and adrenaline, but calmed and relaxed by the alcohol, admitted the murder in the cells, AND fifteen more murders. He stated that he had achieved this by pushing his victims under trains at London Underground Stations on the southern branch of the Northern Line, between Stockwell and Morden. He was asked about the dates, venues and names of the victims, but claimed not to have known any of the victims before the murders. He was unable to elaborate on any details about his crimes.

Upon reflection, the senior detectives formed the opinion that Kelly was lying. "It's all bull---t", was the general view. But they all agreed that the admissions were far too serious for them not to be investigated. An officer was immediately despatched to the offices of the *South London Press*, the local newspaper, in Leigham Court Road just off Streatham Hill. After two days, the officer was able to report that he had discovered a number of reported 'suicides' that matched the confessions made by Kelly. He had, of course, now got dates for these incidents and could now go to Police and Coroner's records for full reports on the same incidents.

The officer was then sent to the Coroner's Office to check their records and more and more complete records were found of deaths that tallied with Kelly's confessions. The senior detectives remained sceptical.

Then the same officer was tasked with checking Kelly's Criminal Record Office (CRO) file and what he discovered left little room to doubt Kelly's confession. Kelly was a small time petty thief. Every year he was sentenced to imprisonment. He would spend 18 months in prison, come out for two days and two people would commit suicide on the Northern Line. He would then be sentenced to 3 years imprisonment and come out for one day and one person would commit suicide on the Northern Line. Every time that he was out of prison somebody would commit suicide. The officer reported back to his senior colleagues, who started to believe that Kelly had been telling the truth.

Finally, the officer went to the British Transport Police Headquarters in Tavistock Square in the West End of London and checked their files. What he found left absolutely no room for doubt. All the files showed a Mr Kieran Patrick Kelly as a witness for each and all of the reported 'suicides'. Apparently, Kelly had waited around at the scene of each of the incidents and spoken to the officer in charge of reporting the incident.

Kelly would tell the officer that he had been standing on the platform of the Northern Line when the man involved in the incident started talking to him and telling him that his wife was being unfaithful to him and that he just could not carry on any longer. As the train came into the station, the man jumped under the front wheels and committed suicide, but there was nothing that Kelly had been able to do to stop him. An investigation showed that in thirty years, Kelly was the only person to have been approached in this way by a person committing suicide and yet he had been approached no less than sixteen times. He was never able to explain these coincidences.

In the Metropolitan Police all files are sent to a General Registry situated near New Scotland Yard. There, all the details of individuals named in the report, their addresses and vehicles are indexed, so that patterns and people who are regularly named in files, can be easily identified. This would have drawn attention to Kelly after the second or third incident, rather than allowing him to function as a serial killer for over thirty years.

In one stroke, Kelly's actions had ruined the life of the poor wife of the deceased. She had lost her husband because Kelly had murdered him. She had lost the family's breadwinner and the insurance company, who had been taking her premiums for several years, refused to pay out on the insurance policy because the husband had committed suicide. Frequently, these financial difficulties lead to the family losing their home and quality of life. Finally, her reputation was ruined by Kelly's comments that the man had claimed that his wife was unfaithful to him.

Now a full enquiry was established. The first task was to secure possession of all the case files and exhibits in all sixteen cases. Most of the case files were held at the Public Record Office in Kew in Middlesex. The forensic exhibits were a bit more of a problem, with thirty-year-old blood and semen stained exhibits, major health hazards that required special protective measures to be in place before they could be safely handled.

CHAPTER 8

Kieran Patrick Kelly

Kieran Patrick (Nosey) Kelly was an enigma. He was a homophobic homosexual. Born and brought up in a small, close-knit community in a rural outskirt of Dublin, to a strict Roman Catholic family, he knew that homosexuality was viewed as a serious sin that led to eternal damnation.

This was a different age from today. Homosexual activity of any type was a crime and homosexuals were frequently attacked in the street, with few police officers or judges particularly interested in stopping such attacks. This was not a time of sexual equality, civil partnerships and same-sex marriages. If Kelly's family had been told of his preferences, they, and all his friends, would have cut him off. His employment opportunities would have been severely limited and his prospects generally poor.

Nosey claimed that he had been enrolled in the Irish Republican Army (the IRA) at birth, so it is also incongruous that he decided to make the trip to London to celebrate the Coronation of Queen Elizabeth II in 1953 (Republicans do not usually attend coronations, unless it's to bomb them!) He met up with a friend, also from Dublin, and did what Irishman have done throughout history, and explored the local pubs.

It was on his way up to Central London on a drinking spree that Nosey's friend made the fatal mistake of pointing out that Nosey had reached the grand age of 30 years without getting married and that he needed to do something about it. There is no evidence that he meant anything by his comment other than to encourage Nosey to settle down, get married and start a family. Unfortunately, for him, Nosey heard something more, he heard that he was being called "a raving puff" and realised immediately that his friend had discovered his greatest secret.

Nosey later reported that he believed his friend was letting him know that he had worked out that he was single because he was homosexual and did not like women. He said nothing more about this topic for the rest of the day, but it troubled him deeply. His friend, coming from the same village, knew all his family and was clearly planning to let them in on his secret. Otherwise why would he have warned Nosey?

The two men travelled up to Central London on the London Underground for "a good drink". They picked up a couple of prostitutes and drank heavily. They got back on the London Underground, together with the two prostitutes that they had picked up, on the last train of the night, to make their way back to their lodgings in Tooting, South London.

It was whilst waiting on the Northern Line platform at Stockwell Station (the same station where half a century later, in 2005, the Brazilian plumber, Jean-Charles de Menezes would be shot by the Metropolitan Police in Operation Kratos) that the solution to his problem came to Nosey. As the train approached the platform, Nosey reported seeing a blinding flash and pushed his best friend to his death under the train. The prostitutes did not stick around to tell their story, but disappeared in the chaos. Nosey then fought his way through the crowds and out of the station.

Unfortunately, the dye had been set and Kelly had set out on a course of action that he could not control and which would dominate his next thirty years.

After killing his best friend, Nosey did not return to his digs, but lived rough for two weeks before daring to return to his family in Dublin. He kept his head down for a month, waiting for a visit from the Police, before thinking about the future, and daring to return to London, where, ironically, he felt that he would be safer because of the larger crowds.

For the next thirty years, Nosey lived in South London, as part of the large homeless community, sleeping in squats, in homeless hostels, or sleeping in parks and open spaces such as Camberwell Green, Kennington Park, Clapham Common and Tooting Common, but also spending most of each year in prison for petty offences of dishonesty, violence and drunkenness.

Nosey was single, unemployed and spent most of his time drinking with a wide circle of friends. He supported himself by thieving, shoplifting, walk-in thefts, petty burglaries and the occasional thefts from motor vehicles. He usually had enough money to buy a drink, although seldom had the money for food. His health was not good.

He was able to fulfil his lustful desires both inside and outside of prison by finding weak men who would let him use them, but who were made fully aware of the extreme violence that they faced if they ever spoke of their relationships with him. When later questioned by Police, his friends all claimed that they were aware that he was homosexual, but did not know the identity of any of his sexual partners.

In 1982 Nosey was arrested and charged with Murder, when a lawyer, an accountant and a doctor were waiting for a London Underground train at Tooting Bec Station and saw Nosey push a man under a train, killing him. Police were unable to show any relationship between the two men, or any motive for the crime, so he was acquitted.

It was just a few months after this acquittal that Kelly was arrested on Clapham Common and taken to Clapham Police Station, where he killed his fellow prisoner in the cells and admitted all his crimes.

CHAPTER 9

The Investigation

When any murder takes place there is a rush to preserve the scene, to collect exhibits and to record the names of all witnesses to the incident. When the death is a death in custody the pressure is intense and all available resources are drawn into the enquiry. So it was in this case. After a few hours things were starting to calm down. The fact that the scene of the alleged crime had been inside a Police Station helped and meant that nobody had too far to travel, or too much difficulty finding their way to the scene of the crime.

The second stage is to collect statements from those people who have been identified as witnesses and to process the exhibits that have been collected. In this case there was also a need to trace those people who had been identified as witnesses to all of the previous incidents which Kelly admitted, and to take updated statements from them and to have all the exhibits from the earlier incidents re-processed.

Over the thirty years since 1953, forensic science had made many considerable advances, not least of which has been the establishment of DNA as a major form of evidence. Consultations were arranged for officers to meet with forensic scientists at the Metropolitan Police Laboratory in order to discuss what further analysis could be undertaken on the old exhibits. New correspondence needed to be submitted seeking that the additional analysis be authorised and funded.

Every witness who had made a statement to the original enquiries then needed to be traced so that new, updated statements could be taken, typed and checked against the original, hand-written statement. Contact details needed to be updated for when these witnesses needed to be warned to attend court to give evidence.

Where witnesses could not be traced, it was necessary to review the evidence in the case in order to identify new witnesses who could cover the material lost. This was painstaking work involving visits to neighbours, checks of voters' registers and tracking back through employment records.

In the days after his arrest, the senior detectives who had spoken to Kelly about what had happened in the cell, were left wondering what it all meant. Had he been telling the truth? Had he really murdered sixteen people? What sort of person was he? Could he really have got away with this sort of behaviour for thirty years? What had gone wrong? What did they need to do to sort this out?

Clearly, it was the first murder, the one that occurred just before the Coronation that dominated Kelly's thoughts. This was the one that he could not explain, even to his own satisfaction. Why had he killed his best friend on a night out? The technique of pushing somebody under a tube train was the same technique that he had employed on most of his other murders. It appeared, at least to him, to be significant. He could not give a motive for any of the incidents and it seemed that he was purely repeating the same crime, hoping that by doing so, he would understand what had motivated him to commit that first murder.

The detectives had left the initial interview a little bemused. They had not been expecting a confession to the murder in the cell, never mind to another fifteen murders that, as local detectives, they knew nothing about. Bit by bit they came to the conclusion that he was "bull----ing". He had not really killed anybody else. He was seeking fame, even if it was at the price of infamy. Maybe he thought that it would give him status in the places that he frequented, Brixton, Wandsworth, Pentonville or Wormwood Scrubs Prisons, or in the parks: Clapham, Kennington or Tooting Common?

Then the thought occurred to them that maybe he had not committed the murder in the cells? Maybe that was all part of the same storytelling? Ironically the confession to the other fifteen murders had raised doubts about the first murder.

Then the facts began to be established. The Forensic Medical Examiner (FME) expressed the opinion that the confession to the murder in the cells neatly fitted with the scientific evidence that had been collected and which was now being processed, so it was probably true. Then the officer checking at the Criminal Records Office at New Scotland Yard started revealing Kelly's long criminal history and among his many cases, there was a recent acquittal at the Old Bailey for a Murder at Tooting Bec Underground Station the previous year – a crime that fitted with Kelly's confessions for pushing people under underground trains.

Drawing the file from the case at Tooting Bec Underground Station, the senior detectives discovered the facts of that case. A man had been pushed under a tube train. The incident had been witnessed by three ideal witnesses, a doctor, a lawyer and an accountant. Each, separately, claimed that they had seen Kelly walk up behind a man standing on the edge of the platform waiting for a train, and stand directly behind him, despite the fact that the rest of the long platform was devoid of passengers. Then as the train came in, and without any discussion or argument, Kelly had simply rotated his shoulder forward. It was a delicate movement, barely noticeable, but it had been enough to launch the man under the train and kill him.

The witnesses were all sane, sober, professionals in good employment and with good character. They were all confident of what they had seen and they each corroborated the others. The case appeared exceptionally strong. At the Old Bailey, however, the defence counsel had questioned why Kelly should want to kill somebody that he had never met. The prosecution had been unable to find any possible link between the two men and without a clear motive, Kelly had been acquitted. It is not recorded how many jury members then made their way home on the Northern Line that evening. Or how many failed to make it home on the Northern Line ...!

Perhaps there was something in Kelly's confession, or maybe he was telling lies. Perhaps he believed that hanging his confession on the story of the incident at Tooting Bec gave it credibility. The matter certainly needed to be investigated.

A decision was then made that the files of the British Transport Police, the people who police the Underground, should be checked for similar incidents up and down the Northern Line for the last thirty years, from the time of the Coronation (1953) to the present day (1983). An officer was sent to their Headquarters in Tavistock Square where he was confronted with rooms full of files. There was no alternative but to plough through them one by one.

Arrangements were made to visit the Metropolitan Police Central Property Store to collect all the exhibits and outstanding property in each of the cases that were being investigated. Then to visit New Scotland Yard to collect all the files on the cases that occurred outside the Northern Line. Detectives then spent days ploughing through the files and briefing themselves on the evidence available and the perceived gaps in that evidence in order that they could advise the Director of Public Prosecutions (DPP) on the strengths and weaknesses of the case and receive his advice on the direction their enquiry needed to take.

After a few days, the officers returned to Clapham Police Station and started ploughing through the files and exhibits that they had collected. The pathologist had, by now, completed the post-mortem and the inquest had been opened and adjourned. The evidence found by the pathologist confirmed Kelly's confession. By now, the senior detectives had consulted with the Director of Public Prosecutions. He had made a decision to charge Kelly with five of the murders to which he had confessed. Five was the number required to classify Kelly as a serial killer.

Seldom is a serial killer charged with all the crimes that he has committed, due to the expense of a courtroom at the Old Bailey, the hire of a judge, prosecuting counsel, defence counsel, a junior barrister and solicitor for each, police officers, security staff, witnesses, etc. The fact that some of these crimes were thirty years old may also have affected his decision, as did the fact that Kelly had been acquitted of the Murder at Tooting Bec and was protected by the law then in force relating to Double Jeopardy.

Five, although a relatively small proportion of the sixteen Murders that Kelly had admitted, was enough to ensure that he was never granted bail. Kelly had appeared at South Western Magistrates Court and been remanded in Police Custody to allow detectives to continue to interview him about developments in the case as they occurred.

It was at this, still relatively early stage of the enquiry that the important decision was made that just one officer should play 'point' in the case and act as the focus of all contact with Kelly. This would allow the officer selected to build a rapport with Kelly and perhaps get to better understand him. The selected officer could also take responsibility for arranging for Kelly to be transported to and from the court and for his weekly remands into custody.

All prisoners remanded into custody have their cases reviewed by the Prison Service at the earliest possible opportunity and Kelly was no different. The Governor-grade at Brixton Prison reviewed the facts of the case and what was known about Kelly from all his recent time spent in prison custody and decided, quite reasonably, that he posed a threat to his fellow prisoners. Accordingly he was classified as a Category A Prisoner.

A Prison Governor is responsible for knowing the exact location of each and every Category A prisoner in his care, so that if the Home Secretary calls, he or she is able to set out his location and state what he is currently doing. At all times the prisoner must be accompanied by two dedicated prison officers, who are unavailable for any other duties apart from ensuring the care, safety and welfare of the one prisoner in their care. Clearly, the Prison Service was not intending to lose Kelly or have him commit any further crimes.

After a couple of weeks, the court decided that Kelly should be returned to regular prison custody and he went to Brixton Prison, which was at that time the regular remand prison, where prisoners were sent for detailed assessment. Each Thursday he had to be collected from Brixton Prison and delivered to South Western Magistrates Court in order that the magistrate could hear any complaints that he had and decide whether his detention was still necessary or whether the time was then right for Kelly to be sent to the local Crown Court, probably the Central Criminal Court sitting at the Old Bailey.

In view of Kelly's Category A status, responsibility for his transport and safety was placed in the hands of the local Metropolitan Police. A special green pyramid-shaped Transit-type van was employed for transporting high-risk prisoners at that time and could frequently be seen speeding between Brixton Prison and the Old Bailey, surrounded by a number of Police Rovers with their flashing blue lights on, and loaded with terrorist prisoners. Kelly did not qualify for the Rovers, but otherwise the service was the same.

In view of Kelly's Category A status and his recent history whilst in Police custody, it was decided that as soon as he arrived at court, his escorting officer would summon the Police Inspector in overall charge of the court and personally advise him of the threat that Kelly posed to his fellow prisoners and advise the Inspector that, under no circumstances should Kelly be detained in a cell with another prisoner. Clearly, no senior officer wanted to be held responsible for another death in custody. The Inspector was then to be required to sign a form accepting that he had been fully apprised of the situation and that he accepted full responsibility for Kelly during his time at the court.

The arrangements to convey Kelly to court were very elaborate and time consuming so when another prisoner from Clapham Police Station was required to be delivered from Brixton Prison to South Western Magistrates Court on the same day, it made sense to arrange both transfers at the same time. The other prisoner had been charged with serious Child Abuse. More on this story later.

Meanwhile, back at Clapham Police Station, enquiries into Kelly's case continued. Files on ten incidents on the Northern Line in which people had fallen under tube trains had been traced. Each one had been recorded as a suicide at the time as there was no evidence to the contrary. In some cases a witness, a Mr Kieran Patrick Kelly, had told Police that the victim, whom he had not previously met, had suddenly started telling him about his wife's infidelity or his financial difficulties and then suddenly jumped under the train as it arrived at the station platform. Unfortunately the BTP did not keep a registry of the names in the files and had failed to identify the frequency with which victims of suicide had unburdened themselves to Kelly.

Further, more detailed enquiries in the archives of the *South London Press*, the local newspaper covering the area, supplied more details of the incidents and filled in some of the gaps in the BTP files. The paper had reported most of the incidents, as well as the inquests that followed.

Kelly's Home Office prison file was traced to the Home Office Prison Department, which was then located at Tolworth Towers on the A3 in Surrey. Disturbingly this file showed Kelly to have repeatedly spent periods of six to twenty-four months in prison, with a day or two out, before he was re-arrested and sentenced, once again, to imprisonment. Over the previous thirty years, Kelly had never spent more than a day or two out of prison. Yet a check of the dates on which the "suicides" on the Northern Line had been committed showed that Kelly had been out for all ten of those identified. This was damming evidence. If he had been lying how could he ensure that he was always out of prison on the days that people jumped under trains?

As the evidence unfolded, attempts were made to re-interview Kelly, but by now he had calmed down and decided to decline to answer any further questions. He had employed a solicitor and, in view of the seriousness of the allegations that he was facing, he unusually got the services of a fully-qualified solicitor at the Police station, rather than those of an outdoor clerk that most prisoners have to settle for.

After a few weeks, the process had become quite comfortable for all concerned. The arrangements to convey Kelly from Brixton Prison to South Western Magistrates Court had been refined and confirmed. Time could be found at both ends of the journey for the officers and Kelly and his solicitor to discuss items of mutual interest. At these meetings, Kelly seldom ate any of the meals provided for him at the expense of the Police Fund, like other prisoners. The detectives in the case took it in turns with Kelly's solicitor to purchase takeaways for all those present. Kelly was supplied with more cigarettes than he could ever hope to smoke by his solicitor and freely supplied them to everybody else, whether a fellow prisoner, a passing solicitor or even a detective. A television set, unclaimed many months after its recovery during another investigation, was set up in his cell, to reduce allegations that Kelly had been placed under duress of any sort. Kelly was (irritatingly!) happier and more comfortable that he had been for years.

The investigation was simple and routine. Some of the witnesses against Kelly had died in the intervening thirty years. Attempts were made to trace alternatives and if this failed, a decision had to be made that certain charges were no longer capable of proof. Four interesting situations remained:

Liverpool Football Club

On another occasion, Kelly could not stop talking about Liverpool Football Club, who were due to play in the European Cup Final that evening. Although he had never been to Liverpool himself, he had many friends amongst the Irish Community who had been, and he felt a firm loyalty to them. He had, in fact, been pestering his solicitor to bring him a transistor radio so that he could, as an unconvicted prisoner, listen to the match in his cell.

Although outraged at the way that Kelly had killed so many people, the officers dealing with him were justifiably proud of the way in which they had treated him, remaining polite and respectful in their dealings with him, listening to all the stories that he told them, in order to gather evidence if possible.

It is not unusual for sex offenders to take pleasure in regaling officers with tales of their exploits, deliberately baiting them to hit them, knowing that if they punched them they were likely to get off and that they would prefer a punch in the face to ten years in prison. The officers dealing with Kelly continually reminded themselves and each other of this fact and each was determined not to be the one to be responsible for letting him off with a punch in the mouth.

The officers were, however, upset at the prospect that Kelly should enjoy such a pleasant evening listening to his favourite football club winning the top prize in European football. After all the pain and suffering that he had caused to his victims and their families, he didn't seem to deserve to enjoy himself. I, the author, was escorting the prisoner that day and having spent the rest of the week talking to the relatives of Kelly's victims, was not pleased to hear quite how much fun he was having following Liverpool's cup run. As the court broke for lunch and Kelly was remanded into custody yet again, his solicitor had to dash away to another court and another defendant. The solicitor suddenly realised that he had forgotten to give Kelly the radio that he had promised to give him to listen to the match on and which unconvicted prisoners on remand are permitted to possess whilst in prison. He asked me to accompany him to his car to collect the radio.

On the way back, the officers could not resist the chance to pull the wire off the speaker before they gave the radio to Kelly. When they gave him the radio he was ecstatic and got very excited at the prospect of listening to the match and being in seventh heaven. Imagine his fury the following week when asked about the match, he had to admit that he had missed it when the radio failed to work. The officers smiled to themselves and thought of all the people that he had killed and felt that they would also enjoy that moment. There was some distress and some small measure of justice for his victims and their families. He never did work out who had 'fixed' his radio so that he missed the match!

Jock Gordon

At an early stage of the enquiry, senior detectives realised that Kelly had long been a senior member of the South West London vagrant community and that there would therefore be a considerable wealth of information about him, his actions and lifestyle that may assist the investigation. Officers had been despatched to make contact and document this information.

Making contact with vagrants invariably means joining their group, which means leaving off washing for a while and bringing a bottle when you visit. Very soon the enquiries revealed vague stories of Nosey Kelly pushing a man under a London Underground train at Kennington Station. Apparently, this man, a vagrant and drunk at the time of the incident, had laid flat between the two rails and allowed the train to go over him. This was important because all the other victims had been killed and, as a result, were no longer available to give evidence. This man could be a valuable witness.

According to the stories, this man had stayed under the train, waited for it to leave and then got back onto the platform. Here, the station foreman, worried that he might lose his job, slapped him about and threw him out of the station. This appeared to the detectives to be rough justice for a man who had done nothing more than been a potential murder victim. In the vagrant community, everybody uses first names or nicknames, and the Police very quickly discovered that this man's name was 'Jock', but nobody seemed to be able to tell them his surname. A considerable amount of money was invested in cider, sherry and extra strong lager in order to find out more information about this man and the incident in which he had become embroiled.

After a few weeks somebody was found who knew the man as 'Jock Gordon', but it was unclear whether Gordon was his first name or surname. After a few more weeks, somebody was found who knew that he lived close to the Oval Cricket Ground in Kennington. Put together, the name of Gordon, the approximate address near the Oval, and the fact that the man was Scottish, was enough to take to the Department of Social Security offices in Marshalsea Road in Southwark, where all the files of vagrants in this country are held. These enquiries led to a Mr Gordon McLintock, who did indeed have a basement flat in Brixton Road in Brixton, not far from the Oval.

This address was kept under constant observation for four weeks before this Gordon McLintock staggered home at the end of a very serious binge, very drunk. He was arrested and taken to Kennington Police Station for being Drunk and Incapable. Twenty-four hours later, with the benefit of a good sleep, three square meals, plenty of liquids to drink and a good shower, Gordon McLintock felt ready to talk about what had happened at Kennington Underground Station.

McLintock was 60 years old and readily admitted that he had spent the last thirty years of his life as a vagrant and that he was friends with the group of vagrants who moved between Kennington Park, Camberwell Green, Peckham Rye and Clapham Common. He stated that he had known Kelly for most of that time and that when in alcohol, they would have some serious fights and inflict quite serious injuries on each other; injuries that would not hurt until days later when they sobered up.

McLintock's memory leading up to the incident at Kennington was very hazy and clearly affected by the fact that they had been drinking together for several days. He was unable to recall exactly what the argument had been about, but it had developed into a fight and he clearly remembered Kelly pushing him under the train on the Northern Line. This was where his memory suddenly improved. Clearly, the recognition that he was in serious danger of being murdered, had caused him to make a very swift recovery from his drunken state.

Gordon had not known what to do for the best, but he had laid flat and a few minutes later the train drove away from the platform. A crowd quickly gathered and the station staff were summoned. The station manager assisted him back onto the platform, but then launched into a tirade, slapped him around a bit and escorted him out of the station. No record of the incident could be found in any London Underground or British Transport Police file. Clearly, the station manager was worried that this incident would reflect badly on the station staff and simply wanted it to go away. Gordon had then made his way home to sleep it off.

Gordon was visited at Kennington Police Station and a full statement taken from him about the incident. He stated that he would be happy to attend court and give evidence against Kelly, particularly when he saw the list of people that Kelly had been charged with murdering, as he had known many of them and several had been good friends.

In the same way that his friends knew Gordon McLintock only as Jock, he knew Kelly only as 'Nosey' Kelly. Despite living together closely for the best part of thirty years, they had no idea of the other's first names. For this reason the DPP required the Police to hold an identification parade in order to ensure that the man that he knew as 'Nosey' Kelly was the man that the Police had charged in the name of Kieran Patrick Kelly.

The law requires that an Identification Parade consists of twelve people of similar height, weight, build and appearance, with spares in case of any objection by the suspect or his legal team. Arrangements were made for the Parade to be held at Cedars Lodge, a home for the Homeless in Cedars Road on the north side of Clapham Common near Clapham Junction British Rail Station.

As the residents were usually required to vacate the premises after breakfast, arrangements were made for the parade to take place at 11 am. Police officers addressed the residents at an assembly after breakfast and explained what they required from the residents. As many of these men knew Kelly and had shared a drink with him at some time, and knew one or more of the victims, they were more than willing to assist with the parade. Twenty residents, who resembled Kelly in height, weight, build and appearance, were selected for the parade.

Identification Parades are difficult to arrange because various people need to enter or leave the room where the parade takes place, but it is important that some of these parties are not permitted to see each other before the parade takes place as this would be likely to influence any witness identification of suspects.

Kelly's legal team had to be shown the room in which the parade was to take place, so that they could check that it was suitable for the purpose, with adequate lighting and room and sufficient doors to allow access and egress. They were invited to comment on the room's suitability and on the route that would be taken by each of the people attending the parade. They had no objections to the room or the proposed routes.

The lawyers were then taken out of the room so that the twenty men who would form the parade could be brought in. As the defence legal team might still raise issues about the arrangements at the trial, it is essential that all the members of the parade are identified so that the parade may be re-formed at the trial for consideration by the judge or jury. It was essential to secure the members' names, addresses and dates of birth of each member of the parade. As these men were of no fixed abode, their criminal records were checked, as these would allow them to be identified and traced should that be necessary for the trial. These men had all been frequently arrested for drunkenness and every one of them knew his own CRO number, having heard it recited every time they had been arrested.

Each man was then provided with a cup of tea and a slice of cake and the £5 note that the regulations allow to be paid to all people who stand on parades. As might be expected, police regulations require a receipt to be obtained from each of the recipients, although several of them were not able to read or write, so there was a long list of 'X's in place of signatures.

Having enjoyed a pleasant cup of tea and a slice of cake, and with a £5 note in their pockets, the members of the parade were very happy and very cooperative. They stood in line as Kelly's legal team came back into the room in order to check them over and ensure that they were happy with the police selection of the men in the parade. This time, three of the men raised objections and were escorted from the room where they would play no further part in the identification parade. As they were allowed to keep their £5 note, they raised no objections to this.

Regulations required that all Identification Parades be conducted and supervised by a uniformed Police Officer of the rank of Inspector, with no connection with the case. In the Metropolitan Police, this officer is provided with an aide memoire in order to assist him or her with his or her responsibilities during the parade. It was at this time that the appointed Inspector, a man of about 45 years of age, entered the room and took charge of the proceedings. He confirmed the selection of the room, the routes to be taken by each party, and then left to go to the ante-room in which Kelly's legal team had been placed, to confirm their agreement with the arrangements.

At this time, arrangements were made for Kelly to be delivered to Cedars Lodge. As he had been charged with most of the murders and remanded in custody to Brixton Prison, he was a Category A prisoner and the Governor of Brixton Prison had to be able to immediately give his location and what he was doing to the Home Secretary if required to do so. A group of four officers in a special prisoner transport vehicle had been despatched to Brixton Prison to collect him and deliver him to Cedars Lodge. When they arrived they remained in the van and used a local radio to call the Inspector in charge of the parade to secure their instructions. He had Kelly delivered to the room and arranged for his legal team to join him there.

Kelly's legal team greeted him and explained the arrangements for the parade and related the objections that they had made to three of the men on the parade. He agreed their actions and expressed his formal satisfaction with the arrangements.

Eleven of the seventeen remaining candidates for the parade were lined up and reviewed both by the Police Inspector and by Kelly's legal team. Kelly was then invited to join the parade and informed that he could stand wherever he wanted. He chose a spot in the line and the other men shuffled along to allow him to stand where he wanted. Everything was working like clockwork and all the manpower and planning seemed to be working.

Gordon McLintock was then delivered to the room from an ante-room on the instructions of the Police Inspector. The Inspector thanked him for coming and asked him to look along the line of men to see whether the man who had pushed him under the train at Stockwell Underground Station was present or not. And that's where the planning was forgotten and it all went wrong!

Gordon took one pace forward and immediately recognised the man who had pushed him under the train and who had killed some of his best friends and punched him squarely in the face. As Kelly hit the floor, all the other friends of the other victims, the men who had made up the parade, all turned on Kelly and started kicking and punching him. The Inspector stepped forward with the intention of stepping in to stop the brawl, but also intending to complete the formalities of the Identification Parade.

Doing his best to be heard above the commotion he said, "Is there any doubt in your mind? Are you certain that this is the man?" Eventually, all the police officers in attendance at Cedars Lodge, and all the social workers on duty, had to step in to stop the violence and separate the parties. It took nearly fifteen minutes to break up the fight. Several people appeared to be convinced of Kelly's guilt.

At court the details of the Identification Parade were quickly related to the jury. The Parade was set up, Kelly took his place on the Parade and McLintock came in and unhesitatingly picked out Kelly as the person who had pushed him underneath a London Underground train at Kennington Underground Station. There was no mention of the incidents that then followed as neither prosecution nor defence saw them benefitting their case.

The Attendance at Court of Paul McManus

The involvement of Paul McManus, the third man in the cell at Clapham Police Station, the man who had witnessed Kelly murder his cellmate, in the investigation ended a couple of hours after the murder, when he sobered up and left the station.

However, it soon became clear that it would be difficult, if not impossible, to trace him and inform him of the date of the trial, in order that he could give evidence of what he had seen in the cell.

McManus' lifestyle, moving around from Common to Common and Park to Park, frequently passing out through the effects of drink and drugs, made him very difficult to keep track of. When Police have difficulty keeping track of somebody before a trial, it is usually a defendant and they deal with this by granting this person bail and getting them to sign on at the Police Station every day, so that the Police can keep track of their movements. A decision was made to make similar arrangements for McManus, but as he was a witness rather than a suspect, it was agreed with McManus that if he signed on every day there would be a £1 note left for him in the bail book.

So, every morning at exactly 9 am Paul McManus would walk proudly into Clapham Police Station and ask the young PC on the front counter to sign on in the Bail Book, quoting reference 41/1A. The officer would go to Book 41/1A and would be surprised to find a £1 note stapled to the sheet, but next to it he or she would find a note explaining the circumstances and instructing the officer what to do. McManus would take the note, politely tip his hat to the officer, wish him or her a good day and gleefully leave the station to head for the nearest off-licence for breakfast!

This worked extremely well, so that on occasions, when the detectives needed to speak to McManus they were waiting to personally present him with his £1 note. And Paul was always happy to spare them a few moments to answer a few quick questions on issues that had recently arisen in the case.

Of course, as the date fixed for the first formal test of the evidence against Kelly, the committal at Lambeth Magistrates Court, approached, so the pressure felt by McManus increased. So it was, then, that when the officers went to pick up McManus to take him to court, he had 'scarpered' and was nowhere to be seen. Officers were despatched to all likely hiding places and McManus was eventually traced and delivered to the court, unconscious and covered in urine and vomit, for all to see.

The arrangements made to secure McManus' attendance at court are set out in the next chapter, but the fact that he was in daily contact with the Police kept him calm, kept him local and kept him safe much longer than would otherwise have been the case.

The Attendance at Court of Gordon McLintock

Gordon McLintock was a council tenant in a basement flat in Brixton Road in Brixton, so it should have been relatively easy to keep in touch with him and provide him with the support that he needed to give evidence at court. Unfortunately, he seldom stayed at the flat and even whilst writing his initial statement for the officers, he told them that he was frightened of the consequences of giving evidence against Kelly and wanted police protection.

Eventually, it was agreed that Gordon would stay at Kennington Police Station for as long as he wanted. The next day he was cautioned for the offence of Drunkenness and formally told that he was free to leave the station. Instead, however, at his own choice, he was taken upstairs to a second, unused set of cells that were retained for Public Order emergencies in central London. Here he remained for almost a year.

Efforts were made by the detectives in the case to make him as comfortable as possible. A television was provided and meals were provided. He was warm and dry and most importantly of all, he was safe from Kelly and his friends. Although Kelly was in prison as he awaited his trial, he had many friends who were not, and who might reasonably be expected to attack McLintock on Kelly's instructions from prison.

Gordon McLintock also found the stress of the impending committal too much to bear in the final days and asked to leave the station and was permitted to do so. He was, however, found in time to appear at court and give his evidence.

Without the support of the detectives in the case, neither McManus nor McLintock would have been available to give evidence of the major crimes that they had witnessed and to which the courts should have been aware. The detectives took the action that they felt was necessary to deliver valuable witnesses to the court and to allow them to freely and openly provide the evidence that they had in their possession to the court. I, personally, can confirm that no attempt was ever made to influence either of them. The Defence never asked about the support offered to witnesses and no lies were ever told about it. Some of their efforts to secure an acquittal for Kelly were far more questionable than anything done by the officers. Such is the nature of our criminal justice system.

CHAPTER 10

The Magistrates Court

South Western Magistrates Court

When Kelly was charged, he then had to be placed before the local magistrates court within twenty-four hours, excluding Sundays or Bank Holidays. The local magistrates court for Clapham was South Western Magistrates Court (now Lavender Hill Magistrates Court) at 176a, Lavender Hill, Battersea SW11 1JU. At court he was remanded in custody and sent to Brixton Prison, where all remand prisoners were sent at this time, as it was equipped with a strong Medical Wing and was capable of assessing all inmates, however disturbed or troubled, as many undoubtedly were, particularly when they first arrived.

Kelly, having been charged with murdering a fellow prisoner at Clapham Police Station, was quickly identified as a security risk and classified as a Category A prisoner, so that the Prison Governor had to be able to inform the Home Secretary of his precise location at any time of the day or night, if required to do so.

As an unconvicted prisoner at that time, Kelly was required by law to be produced at South Western Magistrates Court every seven days for his case to be considered by the Magistrate and for the decision on whether or not to grant bail to be reviewed. As a Category A prisoner this meant that special arrangements had to be made to convey him from Brixton to Lavender Hill every Thursday morning between 8 and 9 am using specialist transport and escorts.

"The Tank" a special bullet-proof and bomb-proof large green, pyramid-shaped vehicle approximately the size of a Ford Transit van, with small cells for two prisoners and room next to the cells (just!) for two Police Officers, was used for this journey. Each Thursday morning it would drive up to Brixton Prison and officers would meet the Governor, check the prisoner, sign for him and place him in the tank. They would then turn on the blue lights and two-tone horns and drive, at speed, to Lavender Hill, in order to avoid any ambush or potential rescue of the prisoner. In the back, Kelly would quietly read a book.

This procedure carried on week-in and week-out for several months and after the second week the novelty wore off and the Detective Inspector decided that he could not spare the time to attend all the remands so that junior detectives were left to deal with them. It was during one of these regular remand appearances that it was decided that Kelly should be put up in an Identification Parade.

Having been charged with several murders, including one of a fellow prisoner at Clapham Police Station, Kelly had been highlighted as an exceptional security risk by the officer in charge of his case. This had been picked up by senior officers in the Metropolitan Police who had issued specific instructions about his transfer from Brixton Prison to South Western Magistrates Court and for his detention whilst at the court. These instructions required that, for obvious reasons, Kelly was not to be detained in the same cell as any other prisoner and that he must be checked every fifteen minutes whilst in custody. Upon his arrival and departure from the court, the Police Inspector in charge of the court must personally sign for his transfer.

When Kelly arrived at Brixton Prison his Category A status meant that instead of simply being transported by the usual prison van with all the other prisoners, Kelly had to be transferred by the officers in the case in a specially equipped van. Very quickly, a routine developed, in which the officers in the case went to the Police Garages in Lambeth in order to pick up a van and driver, then drove to Brixton Prison in order to collect Kelly and then drove through the rush hour traffic to the Magistrates Court, arriving before 10 am. Arrangements were then made to meet up with the Court Inspector in order to brief him on the risks associated with Kelly and transferring him to the Inspector's care. The officers then met up with the defence solicitors to discuss any necessary issues before arranging for Kelly to appear before the magistrate. Then the whole process had to be repeated in reverse as Kelly vas returned to Brixton Prison and the van was returned to Lambeth Garage.

The first time that this routine changed was after about six weeks. It was at this point that the previously-mentioned incident took place, in which the police could not resist sabotaging Kelly's radio just before Liverpool Football Club's appearance in the Final of the European Cup.

Soon after that, another prisoner from Clapham Police Station had been placed in Category A and was due to be transferred from Brixton Prison to South Western Magistrates Court on the same day as Kelly. It was arranged to use the same vehicle but to double the number of officers escorting the prisoners. The second prisoner had been charged with serious Child Abuse. Double the usual number of escorts was arranged and the two prisoners were handcuffed together for the journey. They seemed to get on well together and on the journey they exchanged stories of their treatment by the police. The two men quickly bonded and chatted continuously about their shared hatred of the police and sharing their allegation that the police had "stitched them up".

As the van arrived at the court, and the Court Inspector was summoned, each listened as the officer transferring them set out the risk that they posed. "This man is suspected of sixteen murders, including one of a fellow prisoner in a cell at Clapham Police Station. Under no circumstances is he to be placed in a cell with another prisoner." The child abuser listened intently to what was being said.

The child abuser was then introduced to the Court Inspector. "This man is a child abuser. He has seriously injured his two young daughters. He is a Category A prisoner. It is feared that other prisoners are intent on hurting or even killing him and under no circumstances is he to be detained in the same cell as any other prisoner as he might be killed or kill the other prisoner when attacked". Kelly listened intently to what was said.

The Court Inspector accepted responsibility for the two prisoners and signed the necessary paperwork, accepting that he had been made aware of the exceptional risks that they posed. Later, each prisoner was taken into court in turn for their cases to be reviewed and the question of bail to be reconsidered before each was returned to his cell, pending their return to Brixton Prison.

When the time was right, both men were removed from their cells and handcuffed together, but this time, their attitude to each other had changed. The two men, who had got on so well on the way to the court, immediately started arguing. The child abuser was much bigger than the slight Kelly, and as they got to the top of the stairs leading to the van, the child abuser threw Kelly down the stairs. He then stood proudly at the top of the stairs watching Kelly as he fell down the stairs. Whether he had forgotten that he was handcuffed to Kelly, I don't know, but his obvious pleasure at throwing Kelly down the stairs dissipated as Kelly's weight hit the handcuffs and pulled the child abuser himself down the stairs on top of Kelly.

Neither man was seriously injured and both were placed in the van. There they sat next to each other, face-to-face, eye-to-eye, neither blinking as they turned the handcuffs against each other in order to inflict pain on each other.

"Child abuser"

"Murdering scum"

"The people I killed deserved it. I don't pick on innocent children"

"You murdering bastard! You've killed sixteen people. You scum!"

"I may have killed sixteen people, but I've never hurt a little girl. Especially my own daughter. You scum"

"I've never killed anybody"

"You're not man enough to pick on men. You pick on little children. I'll happily make you number seventeen on my list any time you like"

"Not if I don't turn my back you won't."

The repartee carried on like that and then suddenly they both went berserk and attacked each other. Kelly was no respecter of Child Abusers and his fellow prisoner had no time for somebody who killed other prisoners. There was little that we could do to stop it in such a confined space and travelling at speed on blue lights and two tones. Mayhem prevailed.

Clearly, despite admitting his own guilt (although interestingly, neither did when he subsequently went to court for trial) each was outraged by the other's conduct and felt that the other was worthy of utter contempt. It is interesting how we can all find a way to put ourselves top of the pile – whoever you are and whatever you have done, there is always somebody that you can look down on!

When the van arrived at the prison it was noticed that the two men had been grinding the handcuffs that they wore into each other's wrists. They were taken to see the prison doctor who, after examining X-rays of their injuries, stated that they had made grooves on the sides of the bones on each man's wrists. When the handcuffs were removed the two men chatted happily with the escorting officers, so that the original alignments were completely changed on the return journey.

It was at one of these weekly appearances at South Western Magistrates Court that the defence solicitor raised with the court the issue that Kelly had previously been arrested for one of the murders with which he was now charged. Apparently, at some stage of the enquiry, Kelly had been bailed to return to the Police Station, pending further enquiries being completed.

The officer at court that day made enquiries and confirmed through the Criminal Record Office that this was, in fact, the case. Apparently, a group of six vagrants had been drinking heavily together and one man died when he fell under an underground train. The four survivors had all pointed the finger of blame at Kelly and he had been arrested.

Due to the intoxication of the witnesses, it was felt unsafe to charge Kelly with this offence until further enquiries had been made and he had been bailed to return in a few weeks when these enquiries had been completed. Unfortunately, in the interim the four witnesses in the case all met violent and unnatural deaths. This meant that without any witnesses surviving, there was no prospect of a conviction and the case was dropped. As Kelly had never actually been charged with the offence, jeopardy had never attached to it, and there was no problem with his being charged with it now.

Ironically, this comment by the defence led to the current investigation looking at the deaths of the four witnesses to see whether they could be linked to Kelly. Local gossip had it that Kelly had engaged this man in a hard drinking session, during which he had fed him orange juice laced with white spirit. Enquiries revealed that a post-mortem examination had been undertaken in this case and the cause of death determined to be Liver Failure. As the allegation put fear in people tempted to give evidence against him for any offence in the future, it suited Kelly to encourage the gossip. Indeed Kelly confessed to the police that he had committed the murder.

The officers in the present enquiry were unsure whether Liver Failure was related to the consumption of white spirit and decided to interview the pathologist concerned. Enquiries revealed that this pathologist had been at the start of a very promising career at the time of the death being investigated and that he had now, thirty years later, been appointed Home Office Pathologist.

The pathologist was interviewed by detectives from the enquiry. Arrangements had been made for his original notes of the post-mortem to be made available to him and the detectives related the facts as they knew them and produced details of Kelly's confession to the crime and asked whether there was a chance that it was true, or not. The man went pale and could not speak.

Recognising that he was dealing with a lifelong alcoholic, he had jumped to the conclusion that the death was a result of cirrhosis of the liver and that he had failed to conduct an examination of the deceased's stomach contents, a regular, but not very pleasant experience. This meant that he was not in a position to comment on the validity of Kelly's confession.

How many of us are keen to have an error of judgement committed when we were young men, brought to our attention in later life? A lesson to us all, and I am very pleased that the case against Kelly did not adversely affect his career or his reputation.

When news of this reached Paul McManus, he decamped and disappeared from his usual haunts. McManus had panicked, fearing that Kelly might get bail and murder him too, as a potential witness against him. Alternatively, Kelly had always been popular and maybe he had friends who were outside gaol, who might be prepared to do him a favour and murder

McManus. Best not to take chances. Best to run while you have the chance.

Once again, the DSS came to our rescue. Homeless, unemployed men have no way to feed themselves, or even to buy alcohol, which they often prefer to food. Eventually, they have no alternative but to turn to the DSS for funds and that is how we tracked Paul McManus down, at a DSS Office. He was picked up and taken back to Clapham Police Station and locked up whilst he sobered up and he was then reassured that he would be looked after and protected.

This is a serious issue in the criminal justice system. Serial killers tend to focus on minorities such as prostitutes or homeless people. These people live solitary lives, detached from society. It is easy to shoot, stab or kill them at will, in the confident belief that nobody will notice. When people are charged with their murder, the witnesses are invariably other members of the same community and they can easily be disposed of or chased off.

Lambeth Magistrates Court

Around four months after Kelly had been arrested on Clapham Common, been taken to Clapham Police Station, committed the murder in the cells, and this enquiry had swung into action, all the necessary statements had been taken, typed and checked. All the exhibits had been collected, forensically examined and documented. The senior detectives in the case had submitted reports to the Director of Public Prosecutions, solicitors and barristers had been appointed on both sides and had an opportunity to familiarise themselves with the evidence, and we were ready for the trial.

The defence counsel decided to elect for an "old-style" committal, in which all the prosecution witnesses would be heard in full, in front of a reviewing magistrate, who would then decide whether there was a *prima facie* case that qualified to be sent to the Crown Court for trial before a judge and jury. On this occasion the prosecution had to show that it could make out its case in every aspect, but the defence did not have to produce any witnesses at all and could just snipe at the prosecution witnesses and undermine them. It is a general principle of English law that it is the responsibility of the person or body making an allegation to prove it to the required standard of proof.

This process could take several days and accordingly the case was eventually remanded to the old Lambeth Magistrates Court, opposite the Police Section House (barracks for unmarried officers) in Renfrew Road in Kennington. The building is off the beaten track and away from pedestrian or vehicular traffic and was therefore used in the 1970s and 1980s for numerous high-security terrorism cases and other cases likely to result in protracted hearings.

Most magistrates courts have a geographical responsibility for cases that occur within a certain prescribed area, but Lambeth was one of the few that did not have such a responsibility and instead took cases from other courts that they found burdensome because they required high security or took considerable time.

As soon as the date of the committal hearing was announced, arrangements were made to check EVERYTHING. An officer was despatched to check that Paul McManus was still signing on at the Police Station and to make a point of meeting with him and reassuring him that all was well and that he had nothing to fear and to tell him what he must do if he had any problems. This was a time before mobile telephones, but most of the detectives had purchased one of the new-fangled pagers that sat proudly on the belt and allowed people to keep in touch. Paul McManus was given numbers to call at any time day or night in the event of an emergency.

The night before the committal, young detectives arranged to take possession of a number of Police vehicles so as to ensure that they were not used for any other purpose and were available to collect and deliver witnesses and exhibits. Schedules of who was to do what were drawn up. Lists of which officer would take which vehicle to collect which witness from which address were drawn up. Nothing was left to chance. What could go wrong?

A case of this size and importance would require considerable management, and detectives were allocated responsibilities relating to the appearance of witnesses, the management of correspondence, the management of exhibits, dealing with witness welfare and expenses, and so on. A number of people may ask to see documents and exhibits before, during and after a trial. These range from barristers for both prosecution and defence, solicitors for both sides, magistrates, court clerks, witnesses, senior detectives, etc., and any number of stenographers, probation officers and social workers, etc. It is all very well to deliver everything that is requested, but if it is not returned to its correct place when it is no longer required, then it will not be available for the forthcoming trial at the Old Bailey and that case will be lost.

As the date of the committal neared everything was checked, re-checked and checked again, so that nothing could go wrong. Nobody wanted to be responsible for the release of a serial killer and the subsequent danger to the public. Detectives were despatched, according to a prearranged schedule, to collect all of the witnesses who would be required to give evidence at court. As they arrived these witnesses were greeted and provided with a cup of tea and a biscuit. Most of them wanted a chance to discuss their appearance in court with the officer in the case, and the opportunity to ask when they would be required, how long their evidence would take, how the hearing worked, whether they had to sit or stand when giving evidence and any issues about their evidence that troubled them.

As they arrived, each witness was ticked off on a list. Then the message that everybody had been dreading arrived. Paul McManus, the man sharing the cell with Kelly when he murdered his other cellmate, was not where he was supposed to be in order to meet the officer and could not be found anywhere. Clearly, McManus was an essential witness as he was the only witness the Police had who had seen Kelly committing murder. Officers were despatched to search Clapham Common, Tooting Common, Wandsworth Common, Camberwell Green and Kennington Park. Enquiries were made with the local Police Stations and Magistrates Courts to ensure that he had not been arrested. Local hospitals were contacted to see that he had not been involved in an accident.

A call was put out for McManus, who had clearly panicked at the prospect of having to face Kelly across the court and who had probably been taking a drink to solve his worries, the way he did with most of his problems. McManus had been arrested many times by many officers, so hopefully somebody would find him very soon.

The statements and exhibits duly arrived and were laid out in a way that each of them could be immediately found when it was required. It was then that the call was received announcing that McManus had turned up at the front counter at Clapham Police Station demanding his £1 signing-on fee and was currently in the police van being delivered to the court.

When McManus arrived he was in a terrible state. He was flat out drunk and totally incoherent, covered in dirt, urine and vomit. In the normal course of events it was likely to take six hours for him to sober up and probably more to get himself into a state in which he would present as a reliable witness to the truth. The van driver laid him down in the very small court lobby that provided the only means of access and egress to the building and which made the court ideal for high-security cases. He then drove off at speed, in order to avoid being asked to help with McManus.

A few moments later all the major players in the committal arrived at court and each of them, regardless of rank, was required to step over the prosecution's star witness. There was the magistrate, the court clerk, the prosecuting counsel, the defence counsel, the junior counsel, the prosecution solicitor and the defence solicitor ... and so on. Each of them had to step over McManus in order to get into the court. Most of them were highly amused by his appearance and conduct. Of course, the defence team started to make plans for the afternoon, confident that their client would be acquitted and on his way home by lunch time.

The junior detectives, who were proud to be involved in what might eventually prove to be the most important case of their careers, had all taken great care with their appearance and chosen to wear their best suits to court. They were now required to pick up Paul McManus and move him out of the way of the main entrance to the court building.

Before any clear plans as to where to put McManus and what to do with him could be prepared, the Prosecuting Counsel went into blind panic and even proposed to drop the charges. Clearly the priority must be to calm him down and resolve his problems. He had finalised the order in which he planned to call the witnesses and as McManus had witnessed the first murder, the one in the cells at Clapham Police Station, he was due to be first up in twenty minutes. It was then that dramatic action was required. The senior detective calmed the Prosecuting Counsel, took his brief off him and turned it upside down so that his first witness was last and his last witness was first and instructed him to simply reverse the order in which he called his witnesses, so as to retain the logic of the case, but also maximising the time available for McManus to sober up and prepare himself for court.

Then envoys were sent to the nearby police section house, or barracks, to identify and clear a route for McManus to be taken to the bathroom. Clearly, this was not the time for some stroppy Section House Sergeant to have a tantrum and refuse to allow McManus into his domain. When these envoys returned to the court, they carried McManus to the bathroom and removed their court suits in order to undress McManus and place him alternately in scalding hot and freezing cold baths, in order to assist him to sober up. This process was aided by the purchase of a pot of strong black coffee from the Section House canteen, which was then poured down McManus' throat.

In order to remove McManus from the bath, an old roller towel, which was sitting on the bathroom floor waiting to be fitted to the towel dispenser, was co-opted to deal with McManus. The towel was then given to him to dry himself. Unfortunately, he was not yet in a fit state to be able to dry himself without assistance and once again the young detectives were called upon.

The resourceful young detectives then found a cleaner at the Section House who had started work at 6 am and was due to finish at 10 am, but who had been detained at work finishing the tasks assigned to him. He was generously bribed to remove the thick silt from the baths used by McManus and to burn the roller towel that had been used to dry him.

Young detectives were then sent to the local chemist to buy soap, shampoo, razor, comb, tooth paste and tooth brush. Others were sent to the local Oxfam shop to pick up a suit, shirt, tie, shoes etc. When McManus had shaved and washed, he was rewarded with a greasy breakfast and started to feel better. The officers who had been sent to the Oxfam shop returned with a grey pin stripe suit that fitted McManus rather well, but had failed to find the shirt, tie or shoes that they had been sent to find.

Dramatic action was required and one of the detectives went to the Section House Drying Room, where residents put wet clothing to dry after a rainstorm. Here they found a uniform white shirt left there by an officer and which they 'pinched' for McManus. There were no shoelaces lying around, but after careful consideration, McManus' shoes were found to be acceptable and they were put back on his feet.

By lunchtime, McManus was ready to go into court and face the people whom he had amused so recently with his appearance. He was paraded in front of the officer in the case, to check that his appearance was acceptable. He made an interesting exhibit.

McManus was, by this time, upright. He was relatively steady on his feet. His hair had been dried, but it was still damp and had been slicked down with a comb so that it was flat to his face, but the bit on the top of his head just stuck out at the sides. He had shaved and was clean-shaven across most of his face, but the bits of his neck that showed, and the bits around his nose that were a bit fiddly, were still quite hairy. His eyes were very watery and bloodshot and were described at the time as being a bit like "piss holes in the snow". He wobbled as he stood for the inspection.

McManus wore the white police shirt with the grey pinstripe suit. His shirt was open at the neck as he had no tie. He looked quite the professional from the neck down. He would do. It was at this moment that the Detective Inspector arrived at court. He was a former member of the Metropolitan Police Flying Squad, and, told of the lack of a tie on McManus, he returned to his car and returned to the court with a Flying Squad tie, a red tie bearing the motif of a swooping golden eagle that sits just below the collar. It completed McManus' ensemble just as he was called into court at 2 pm as the court returned from lunch to hear his testimony.

McManus was propelled to a position just behind the door to the court. His shoulders were rubbed and he was fed words of encouragement as he prepared to enter the court and face his challengers. The door swung open and, next to the usher holding the door open and calling his name, could be seen an array of faces, all looking to see what was going to happen next, and whether the witness would be ready and sober for his task.

McManus took hold of the rail, steadied himself, briefly tripped on the step up to the courtroom, but then confidently settled himself and walked into court. Every eye in court was upon him. Few were dry. Several people were using handkerchiefs to wipe away tears.

The Queen's Counsel representing both Prosecution and Defence handed the interrogation of McManus to their deputies. These are clever, shrewd men, who have been around the block. They have been here before. They recognised the potential for disaster that McManus posed. Nobody was going to win this one. You grilled the drunk and did what you were paid to do, or he made a fool of you. And you don't want that reputation when you are a Queen's Counsel.

McManus dealt competently with Prosecution Counsel's questions, but that was the easy part. Now for the Defence Counsel and his questions. The first question was posed with sarcasm. It was quickly batted back as McManus pulled himself to his full height and replied, "What you young whippersnappers forget is ..." Defence Counsel was put firmly back in his place and Paul McManus and the entire prosecution team did not look back. From then on there was only one winner and McManus gave the performance of his life and convinced the magistrate that he had seen what he said he had seen, and that Kelly had killed the other prisoner.

Kelly was very swiftly despatched and duly committed to the Old Bailey to stand trial on all charges. The prosecution had lived to fight another day. Now for the Old Bailey! Now for the real deal: five Murder trials in Courts 1 and 2 at the Old Bailey. This is where the case would be won or lost.

The months between the committal and the trial were filled with random questions from Kelly's defence team as they tried to get a good grip of the case and attempted to invent some credible defence to the charges for him.

CHAPTER 11

The Central Criminal Court
at the Old Bailey

The Central Criminal Court is the senior criminal court in England and Wales. It is situated at the junction of Old Bailey and Newgate Street, about 200 yards northwest of St Paul's Cathedral. The word 'bailey' refers to the reinforced wall on the western edge of the City of London that in ancient times separated the City of London from the City of Westminster. The court therefore allowed easy access to both cities and, situated next to Newgate Prison, historically allowed suspects to be tried and executed without delay.

The current building maintains the key features of the design of the original building that have been preserved in each reincarnation of the court. The accused sits in "the dock" or at "the bar" directly facing the witnesses in the case standing in the "witness box" whilst the judges sit in an elevated position on the other side of the court, overseeing the proceedings. This layout creates a sense of conflict between the accused and the rest of the court.

Jurors originally sat around the walls of the court on both left and right of the accused, but since 1737 they have been brought together in two rows of stalls on the right of the accused, where they can consult privately and arrive at verdicts without needing to leave court. This left the court clerks, lawyers and shorthand writers sitting in the well of the court where they were accessible to the judges that they served.

Having been committed to stand trial at Lambeth Magistrates Court, on behalf of South Western Magistrates Court, Kelly faced five charges of murder. Although the prosecution took the view that he had committed sixteen murders, it was felt unnecessary to charge all of these as one conviction would be enough to earn him a sentence of Life Imprisonment. A decision was taken by the Director of Public Prosecutions to

seek to convict Kelly of two murders. In this way a prisoner who
feels that he may be able to secure an appeal on one charge will
not bother as there will always be a second conviction to justify
a term of Life Imprisonment.

By the time Kelly appeared before the Old Bailey in April
1984 it was thirty-one years since the first murder that he
stood accused of, the one where he was alleged to have pushed
his best friend under a tube train at Stockwell Underground
Station. Many witnesses had died, been taken seriously ill,
moved away, failed to see the purpose in pursuing the matter,
and so on and memories had faded. It would never be easy to
secure convictions under these circumstances.

The case was listed for Court 2, before Judge Michael Argyle,
who had sat for many years at the Old Bailey, and who was
never less than interesting. Unpredictable, volatile, right-wing,
deaf to political correctness, he was one of the old-fashioned
judges who are described euphemistically as "robust" and by
disappointed defendants and not a few counsel who appeared
before him as "a dog". Ultimately, with an early retirement in
1988, he paid the price for his views and utterances, but he
remained unrepentant to the end of his life.

Judge Argyle was frequently in the press for the comments that
he made. These included his comment to an attempted rapist on
whom he imposed a suspended sentence: "You come from Derby,
which is my part of the world. Off you go and don't come back."
Others included, "You are far too attractive to be a policewoman -
you should be a film star"; "a vicious little sodomite [homosexual]
from Glasgow," to a mugging victim; and, when a strike had
cancelled television coverage of a Test match in the West Indies,
"It is enough to make an orthodox Jew want to join the Nazi
party." It is Argyle to whom the term "Thiefrow" is attributed,
following a spate of thefts at Heathrow Airport.

It is a paradox that whilst middle class defendants struggle
to find the money to secure even the most basic legal
representation, those unable to feed themselves, when accused
of the most heinous crimes, secure some of the best barristers in
the land, often on a pro-bono (free) basis. So it was with Kelly.
He was represented by Richard du Cann QC, already a senior
Old Bailey Judge in his own right.

Du Cann's obituary in the *Independent* newspaper states that he "made a significant contribution to his profession. What he took from it he repaid in full measure. Few gave more of their own time and energy to the resolution of issues affecting the workings of the criminal justice system. He served as Chairman of the Criminal Bar Association between 1977 and 1980 and as Chairman of the Bar from 1980 to 1981. No Royal Commission which affected the Bar (and there were four of them during his years as Treasury Counsel and as Silk) was complete without a contribution from him, and his opinions were always trenchant and perceptive."

The prosecution suffered a frequent and regular problem with different barristers being employed to conduct each prosecution and never managing to gain the familiarity and knowledge of their opponents.

The trial started with everybody introducing themselves to the court. Whilst the Judge and Leading Counsel on either side probably knew each other very well, it was an opportunity for them to meet their juniors and for the other people in court to meet the cast for the show ahead. The names of those involved in the case made up an impressive list of players.

Next the charges were put to Kelly, who pleaded "Not Guilty" to all charges. Police Officers frequently witness prisoners who have happily confirmed their active participation in crime during an investigation then deny everything to the court.

When the pleas had been recorded, the Defence Counsel rose to make a point of law. He asked for each of the Counts on the Indictment to be heard separately as he felt that his client might not get a fair trial if the jury heard just how many murders his client had been accused of. This was entirely predictable and readily acceded to by the Judge.

We then proceeded to select a jury. The Clerk of the Court called out names and some were rejected and some were questioned until the panel was filled. When the prosecutor objects to a potential juror, he or she proclaims, "Stand by for the Crown". When the defence council objects to a potential juror he or she calls out, "Objection". It is the last time in a criminal trial that the prosecution gets the advantage.

The first trial would be the one relating to the incident in the cells at Clapham Police Station. Paul McManus was the first witness. He gave evidence well and was congratulated by the Prosecuting Counsel. We then worked through a list of Police witnesses ranging from the officers on duty in the Police Station, to the Scenes of Crime Officer, the Fingerprint Officer, the Photographer, the Forensic Medical Examiner, and then the Paramedic called to the scene, the pathologist and the senior detectives who interviewed Kelly. The defence challenged every point and declined to accept any but the most simple evidence in statement form, challenging the prosecution to produce every witness and every exhibit. No witnesses were called for the Defence. Not even Kelly gave evidence on his own behalf.

It therefore came as a shock when the jury announced that they were unable to reach a unanimous verdict. The Judge gave them a formal direction telling them that, under certain conditions, which now applied in this case, he could accept a majority verdict in which ten out of the twelve jurors agreed. The jury returned several times to express the opinion that this would not be possible and eventually the judge accepted this view and ordered a re-trial.

There was a considerable debate about this verdict. Three men in a locked room. One is strangled and as you cannot strangle yourself, it must be one of the other two. The evidence was that Kelly had admitted this to the rapist, then to police. Nobody, not even Kelly or his legal representatives, had ever accused Paul McManus, either before the trial or at the trial and McManus had certainly never confessed to the crime. What *reasonable* doubt could there be?

We started again the next day. A new jury and a new allegation of Murder. The witnesses filed through the court. A few weeks went by and then there was another hung jury, another mistrial. The reason why the Defence Counsel wanted separate trials suddenly became clear. They could make the same allegations against all the witnesses in all the cases, in front of different juries and they would accept it as being justification for reasonable doubt and acquit Kelly. There were four mistrials in a row before a jury found Kelly guilty of Manslaughter. Fears that he never be convicted of Murder were allayed, at least in part.

It was then decided to run one of the mistrials again. As one might expect in a retrial, it was a largely a repetition of what had been said in the first trial. Then, suddenly and without warning, the Defence Counsel called evidence from Kelly that he had been in prison at the time that this murder had taken place.

In law, evidence that the prisoner could not have committed the crime because he was somewhere else at the time it was committed, is known as Alibi Evidence. It is treated with some caution because you can say that you were anywhere else in the world and bring anybody you like to court to support your case, usually a husband or wife or close friend, who might be induced to lie to get the prisoner off.

The law requires that any prisoner proposing to call alibi evidence must serve formal notice on the Prosecution within fourteen days of the committal to the Crown Court. It was now over six months since Kelly's committal and he had already been through one trial for this offence and only now was he informing the Prosecution that he had an alibi.

Judges are always keen to be fair to defendants and to give them the benefit of any doubt and the best possible chance to clear their name, so the judge allowed the alibi evidence to be heard. It was now 11.30 am and the Judge, in an attempt to be equally fair to the Prosecution, gave us until 3.00 pm to produce evidence on which to challenge the alibi. It was not long.

After two years of careful investigation and preparation the case would now stand or fall on what happened in the next two and a half hours. The idea that a serial killer might escape justice by a series of lies and then continue to kill more people was intolerable and the Police Team swung into action.

Urgent calls to the Home Office Prison Department in Tolworth Towers on the A3 in Surrey, were made from the Police Room at the Old Bailey. When the Records Department checked they found that they held no records of Kelly's imprisonment in 1974, but these had been checked only a few months ago as part of this investigation. The reason for raising this defence at this time then became clear. Home Office policy was to destroy all files on the day that they became ten years old.

In this case the files had become ten years old just one week earlier and had been destroyed in accordance with the policy.

If the defence honestly believed that Kelly had been in prison at the time of this offence then surely they would have raised the issue in the earlier trial. But at that time, the files were only nine years and 48 weeks old and not eligible to be destroyed. Clearly, this was a dishonest strategy to secure an acquittal for their client.

As the telephone conversation to the Prison Department continued, more interesting facts came to light. A very small pilot project had been commissioned by the Home Office a few years ago, to look at the feasibility of computerising all the vast prison records. As luck would have it, Kelly's old file had been one of the files that had been computerised and it still existed. Due to the exceptionally small size of the project, nobody ever thought about destroying those files.

The final question was whether this computerised file met the criteria to be classified as an official record so that a Home Office official could refer to it when giving evidence. Enquiries at the Home Office revealed that the procedure employed in the trial required the computerised version to be checked for accuracy not once, not twice, but three times.

It *did* meet the criteria to be an official record and could be used in court by a Home Office official to give evidence and disprove Kelly's alibi. Unfortunately, time was rushing on and it was now 1.00 pm and the court has risen and the counsel dispersed, so there was no legal advice available. There was now just two hours to get a Home Office official to court before the judge was going to throw the case out and let a serial killer lose to kill again ... and again.

Then the next problem was identified. In order for a Home Office official to go to court to give evidence the Police Commander at the Home office, in charge of Department P5 had to give his or her authority. Unfortunately, he was sick and unable to give that authority. His deputy was on annual leave. His assistant was on a course. There was nobody else. It was a small department.

The Home Office official on the telephone was most helpful, but very clear, his job was at risk if he attended court without the necessary authority. So what about going up the organisation. Who outranked the Commander P5? OK, so where's the Home

Secretary today? No solution could be found and it was now 2.00 pm. Just an hour to go.

I, the detective at court, decided to travel down to Tolworth and see what could be arranged. I was satisfied that the release of a serial killer was sufficient emergency for me to drive my Police vehicle in excess of the speed limits and drove there with all haste. I arrived at the Tolworth Towers at 2.30 pm. I met the Home Office official who I had been talking to on the telephone and we sought a solution, but time did not permit this luxury. Without warning, I bundled the Home Office official into the Police car and took off down the A3 at 80 mph. As I did so, I told the Home Office official that he could leave the vehicle at any time, but that it was not recommended.

We arrived at the Old Bailey at 3.00 pm, but it took a few minutes to park the car and run to Court 1. As we arrived I begged for cooperation, but it was declined. I ran into court just in time to hear the judge address the jury on why it was necessary to acquit Kelly. When, after a brief delay, the detective explained the situation the judge issued a warrant for the arrest of the Home Office official, but suspended it for five minutes. He needed about seven minutes to write out the warrant. This just gave the official time to get himself into court and to get ready to give evidence. This was the only excuse that the Home Office official needed. He read from the computerised record and informed the judge that Kelly had, indeed, been free to commit the murder.

Having been caught, so spectacularly lying, the defence could do nothing more than immediately change their plea to one of guilty. The judge accepted the plea and sentenced Kelly to Life Imprisonment. For good measure he thoughtfully commended my actions, to prevent any unnecessary allegations of kidnap and false imprisonment.

The prosecution team, were then faced with one conviction for Murder and one conviction for Manslaughter and decided that they needed to take advice on whether to continue with the mistrials or to bring the case to a conclusion. The DPP instructed them to leave the remained cases on file and bring the trial to a conclusion, which they did.

After six months at the Old Bailey, Kelly was eventually placed in the prison system for the remainder of his natural life.

Although it has not been possible to secure confirmation that Kelly died in prison, this remains the most likely outcome. He would be 91 years old if he was still alive today.

CHAPTER 12

The Conclusion

Kieran Patrick Kelly had nobody to talk to after the incident in the cells at Clapham Police Station. He had lived alternately as a member of the local homeless community and as a prisoner in local South London Prisons for thirty years, but when he murdered a homeless man in a Police cell he had turned both communities against him.

In place of his old friends, he had a junior detective, a young man, as the only person prepared to speak to him and the only person that he could talk to for his needs, such as cigarettes or sweets or reading materials, writing materials, etc.

We were both trying to understand what happened and why it happened and in order to make sense of it all Kelly opened up to me during our hours together. Although he would never admit it either to himself or to others, it appeared clear to me that he was suffering from a severe case of homophobia. He struggled with a homosexual attraction to other men that his culture, his faith and his beliefs told him was wrong.

I spoke to a number of men who claimed to have had a brief sexual relationship with Kelly, but all told the same story of rejection and denial shortly after his needs had been gratified. When I brought these allegations to Kelly they were met with an unnaturally fierce denial.

Living in Dublin, in a close-knit community of family and friends it would have been impossible for Kelly to explore his sexuality, and it appears that he was able to keep it in check.

In London, in a place where nobody knew him and there was greater freedom, he was able to explore his sexuality more fully and gratify his needs.

The problem came to a head when Dublin met London and one of his old friends from Dublin made a comment about why he was not married and whether he just didn't like women. Kelly could not cope with that and he may well have feared that his friends would return to Dublin and tell all his family and friends of his secret.

Something had to be done to stop him. To reason with his friend, to plead with him or simply to beg; all these acts would have confirmed the suspicion and made it even more likely that his secret would get out.

The alternative was to kill the secret by killing the person holding it. When his friend died under the tube train the secret died with him and for a while at least, Kelly was safe.

Although Kelly was safe after killing his friend, he struggled with guilt about what he had done. Because he denied the truth about why he had done what he did, he struggled to understand it and, unable to understand it, he could not deal with it.

He had no reason at all for killing all those people on the Northern Line; he had never seen them before; he didn't know anything about them. On many occasions he walked up behind perfectly innocuous, innocent, bland members of the public and gently rotated his right shoulder, so that it pushed them gently forward and, standing too close to the edge of the platform as we all do, they simply fell under the train.

Kelly grew in confidence with each crime that he committed. After killing his friend, he ran away immediately and spent the next few weeks looking over his shoulder, expecting the Police to come looking for him. After a few more attacks, he waited around for the Police to arrive and delivered carefully prepared stories of how the victim had discussed his personal problems, his wife's infidelity and his financial difficulties.

His stories reveal that he enjoyed the power that the murders gave him. Power over his victims, and the power to deceive. This is confirmed by the pleasure that he took in relating the entire story of the sixteen murders to the senior detectives who interviewed him. Because the murder in the cell was so recent he had not regained his composure after the attack and was still freshly reliving the pleasure that it had given him.

As a result of the stories told to the British Transport Police Officers who investigated the murders on the Northern Line, the insurance companies elected not to pay out, as is their right in cases of suicide. So, as well as depriving the families of their loved one and taking away the family breadwinner, he also stopped them receiving their justified compensation for their loss. Many families faced penury as a result. As part of my work, I made a point of contacting the insurance companies in each of the cases that we investigated and made them aware of what had happened. I was then able to apply pressure to ensure that all the families received the compensation to which they were entitled and from which they had been defrauded by Kelly's actions. It seemed to be the least that we could do after what they had been through.

So what can be done to ensure that nothing like this happens again? Very likely, as society moves on and we all work longer hours and put ourselves under greater and greater pressure, there will be more and more serial killers. Hopefully, as a result of this case and the rise in computer technology, police forces around the country will keep a record of the people with whom they come into contact, so that when one person continually witnesses suicides or murders, consideration can be give as to whether there is a deeper problem that needs looking into. If that had happened in this case, perhaps Kelly would have been stopped after three or four murders, rather than being allowed to keep going to sixteen.

Index